YOUR GENDER BOOK

by the same author

The Book of Non-Binary Joy
Embracing the Power of You
Ben Pechey
Illustrated by Sam Prentice
ISBN 978 1 78775 910 7
eISBN 978 1 78775 911 4

of related interest

It's Totally Normal!
An LGBTQIA+ Guide to Puberty, Sex, and Gender
Monica Gupta Mehta and Asha Lily Mehta
Illustrated by Fox Fisher
ISBN 978 1 83997 355 0
eISBN 978 1 83997 356 7

Perfectly Queer
An Illustrated Introduction
Victoria Barron
ISBN 978 1 83997 408 3
eISBN 978 1 83997 409 0

LGBTQIA+ Pride Sticker Book
Illustrated by Ollie Mann
ISBN 978 1 83997 246 1

Queer Body Power
Finding Your Body Positivity
Essie Dennis
ISBN 978 1 78775 904 6
eISBN 978 1 78775 905 3

Your Gender Book

Helping You Be You!

Ben Pechey

Illustrated by Sam Prentice

Jessica Kingsley Publishers
London and Philadelphia

First published in Great Britain in 2024 by Jessica Kingsley Publishers
An imprint of John Murray Press

1

Copyright © Ben Pechey 2024
Illustrations Copyright © Sam Prentice 2024

The right of Ben Pechey to be identified as the Author of the Work
has been asserted by them in accordance with the Copyright,
Designs and Patents Act 1988.

Front cover image source: Sam Prentice.

A CIP catalogue record for this title is available from the British
Library and the Library of Congress

ISBN 978 1 83997 610 0
eISBN 978 1 83997 611 7

Printed and bound in Great Britain by Bell & Bain Limited

Jessica Kingsley Publishers' policy is to use papers that are natural,
renewable and recyclable products and made from wood grown
in sustainable forests. The logging and manufacturing processes
are expected to conform to the environmental regulations of the
country of origin.

Jessica Kingsley Publishers
Carmelite House
50 Victoria Embankment
London EC4Y 0DZ

www.jkp.com

John Murray Press
Part of Hodder & Stoughton Limited
An Hachette UK Company

For all those who came before, and all those yet to come.

In memory of my Grandpa, who always believed in me.

Contents

Preface 9

Introduction 11

1. Gender, Sex and Sexuality 13

2. The Lion, the Witch and the Gender Identities in the Wardrobe 25

3. Pronouns Aren't People 35

4. Question Time 47

5. I'm Not Sure, and That's Okay! 57

6. Feeling Lonely? Read This! 65

7. What's in Your Wardrobe? 75

8. A Town Called Barriers 87

9. When Was the Last Time You Were Happy? 99

10. How to Support Your Friends 109

11. What Next? The Start of Your Gender Story 119

12. Things I Wish I Knew 129

13. Useful Resources 143

This Isn't Goodbye Really 155

Acknowledgements 159

Puzzle and Questions Solutions 161

Notes 169

Preface

Writing a book is not easy. Sure, hundreds of people have done it, but that doesn't stop the blank page in front of you feeling super-scary sometimes. Trust me. As a writer, I know that some days it can be a struggle to get just ten words out. However, I have been very lucky with the books I have written.

Lucky, because unlike other authors, I knew exactly why I was writing. Both my first book and now this exciting book you're holding have had a very clear purpose. That purpose has been to help. To do my best to make sure whoever reads my words feels better because of it.

This book is so important to me because of how many people, like myself, grew up without help like this. Generations of LGBTQIA+ people have come and gone, and yet we are still struggling as a community!

The world is having an identity crisis. People who experience gender in different ways are coming under fire from pretty much every corner. It can feel very confusing right now to be LGBTQIA+, especially for gender-diverse and trans people.

Writing this book has shown me that my job is not to do it for myself. Very sadly, I cannot undo the harm that happened in my early years. I cannot change that my childhood was spent not being the person I am now. We didn't have the language, the understanding. The world was a harder place for members of the trans community.

I know I cannot change any of this – but I know that I have a role to play to ensure that future generations do not have to struggle as so many people have done in the past. I must also mention that my life has been exponentially improved thanks to the tireless work of the community long before I even thought I could help. I am so grateful to be standing on the shoulders of giants, continuing the legacy of their work.

In sharing my words, I hope to put them into action. So, whoever you are, thank you for picking up this book and taking in my words. My only hope is that we can create a world with a little more acceptance and peace for LGBTQIA+ community members. We just want to live our lives. Reading this book can – in a small way – be the first step.

Introduction

This book is first and foremost for you. Hello and welcome. Please make yourself comfy. The pages of this book are a safe space. There is no judgement. No fear. Most of all, there is only support for you.

I have never fitted in. In some ways this has been a good thing. However, for a long time not fitting in made my life very difficult. Coming to this book, you may be worried that you don't fit in! Well, don't worry – you are in very good company!

Life is presented to us with lots of 'rules' – we should act in a certain way; we should all want the same things. This is very silly. If we were all the same, nothing new would ever happen. If we all acted the same, imagine how dull life would be.

A good example of this is that professional people should look professional to be taken seriously. Politicians are told off if they don't dress smartly! Well, let me tell you, I am a professional writer (look, mum, I made it!), and I wrote most of this book wearing pyjamas! Sometimes good things happen when we approach them differently.

Doing things differently is celebrated in this book. Which means *you* are celebrated here! The topic of gender is what has brought us together because it is a big deal. Our gender expression and identity is one of the main ways we are viewed and understood by others. So it can be scary to take a different approach to it.

These pages hold possible ways you can have a better life. The book is a guide, rather than an instruction manual. I cannot understand all experiences or circumstances. If I could, I would be a genius! Instead, I can offer you my life experiences and emotional support to help you get to grips with who *you* are.

If you are here, it is because you want to learn more about your gender. Maybe you want to learn more about gender so you can understand other people more. Maybe you are just curious. Whatever the reason, everyone is welcome. Gender is something we all need to get our heads around. Gender is connected to pretty much everything:

- Gender can be still.
- Gender can be fluid.
- Gender can be nothing.
- Gender can be everything.
- Gender can be confusing.
- Gender can be colourful.
- Gender can be black and white.
- Gender can be anything you want it to be...

This book is here to hold your hand, to answer your questions, soothe your soul, and help you understand yourself in new ways. The best place to start is at the beginning. The best time is now! So turn the page and let's explore who *you* are!

Chapter 1

Gender, Sex and Sexuality

Gender has become a big deal. It is silly, really, how much fuss some people make about it. If less fuss was made, I think more people could be happier. As you read this, you will notice some patterns. The first is that people who make the most fuss about gender are the ones who are the most comfortable with their own gender identity. This is a pattern that will pop up over and over – other people's opinions.

Whether this book is for yourself or for a friend, this chapter is very important.

In this chapter we will:

- Explore the confusing world of gender together.
- Investigate what all of this could mean for you, and for the people around you.
- Look at the link between gender, sex and sexuality.
- Oh, and, of course, we can't forget the wider world we live in!

This is the perfect place for you to start. The rest of the book will make more sense after reading this bit. Think of this chapter as the walls of the house. The walls don't make a house cosy or comfortable, but a house can't stay standing without walls! We need the walls before we can make a house warm and lovely. So – don't skip this bit. It will help make what follows easier to understand.

Let's Talk about Gender

It makes sense to start at the beginning. We need to really grasp what gender is. Gender is a twisty thing – like holding on to a snake. It moves around a lot, changes, and likes to keep you on your toes. However, this snake is not harmful. Gender is part of all our lives, and when handled correctly, it is actually lovely.

Gender is who you are as a person. This means how you feel inside, your identity as a person. Some people feel like a girl; some may feel like nothing; some will feel like a boy; and others may be confused. This is all part of gender. It is not about parts of our body. Instead, our gender is how we feel as people. This is why gender is different for all of us.

Gender expression is also part of this. The way we express our gender is part of how other people see us. What we do and how we do it is how we show who we are. Sometimes we can display our gender through the things we choose to wear. There are words that can help us explain this expression.

You can describe yourself as feminine, masculine (which are easy enough), or androgynous – which means a wonderful unique blend of gender expression. There are plenty of other ways to describe yourself, which we will cover later on.

It can feel like a huge thing to have to experience and explore. For some people it is very simple. However, some of us need to take a little more time to work out who we are – and this is completely okay. I am still doing it too!

The Physical Part

If gender is the way we feel about ourselves, then we have to cover the physical part. When we are born our sex is based on external genitalia – the bits doctors can see. This is a girl or a boy. There are a lot of gender identities, but only two sexes, according to science. When there are only two options, we call this binary. So, male and female, boy and girl, man and woman – these are all binary sexes.

Unlike your gender, your sex is not something you can control. This is the way our bodies are formed in the womb – a little like a body lottery. The next sentence is very important, so maybe you want to underline it (but not if it's a library book!). Your assigned sex does not define *you*. This means that your body does not make the rules. You don't have to express a certain gender identity because of how your body looks – just because you have boy parts or girl parts *does not always mean that is who you are*.

It is very possible that you do not feel that your sex is the same as your gender identity or expression. This is okay, and we will be exploring this together in depth a little bit later on. We hear and see the word 'normal' written a lot. No one knows what 'normal' really means. No one can ever say that they're fully 'normal' – because 'normal' doesn't exist. So worrying about your gender identity not matching your body parts is something you don't need to do.

A Note on Intersex

Nurses and doctors use our physical characteristics to determine our sex when we are born. Some people are born with variations of external body parts. This means that intersex people have bodies that do not fit typical definitions of female and male. Intersex people can be born with some body parts we expect boys to have. Intersex people can be born with some body parts we expect girls to have. Intersex people can be born with some traits and body parts that most boys and girls don't have all in the same body.

People who are intersex have small differences, inside and out, which are different to others. It also means that intersex people's bodies work differently to others. Intersex people don't fit into the same category as those who have binary assigned sex – boys and girls. We are all different, and being intersex is just a small part of this. Difference is not bad – it is what makes us unique.

Being intersex is also not a gender. Some intersex people identify as women, some identify as men, and some say they are intersex, and they may also identify as trans or non-binary. We have already discovered that our gender is not the same as our assigned sex. It makes sense that those who are intersex have varying gender identities and expressions.

Some people who are intersex feel at home within the LGBTQIA+ community. Some intersex people don't feel they belong there. It is an individual thing for each intersex person to decide!

Who Do You Like?

As we develop as people, we begin to form bonds with others. Some people call these crushes. My first crush was TV chef and presenter Ainsley Harriott! We cannot help who we have crushes on, or indeed who we fall in love with. Just like our gender identity, it is part of who we are, and is just how we feel.

As you have probably realized, other people get caught up in who people choose to love. This is why we have labels for the types of people we have romantic feelings towards. This label is our sexuality. There are quite a few, and the easiest way is to list them for you:

- Lesbian – girls who are attracted to girls.
- Gay – boys who are attracted to boys, which can also be called homosexual.
- Bisexual – people who are attracted to both girls and boys.
- Heterosexual – people who are attracted to the opposite sex – girls who are attracted to boys and vice versa.
- Asexual – people with low or no sexual desire for others. However, asexual people can form romantic attachments.
- Pansexual – a person who is not attracted to any particular gender, sex or sexuality. Instead, they focus on people they like for who they are.

Just like with your assigned sex, your sexuality does not make you who you are. There are lots of behaviours associated with certain sexualities. These behaviours are not something you have to aspire to be like. As with all of these categories, you always get to be in charge. It is also worth saying that our sexuality is not fixed. Like so many aspects of our lives, as we grow, things don't stay the same. So your sexuality can change and develop over time too.

The Link between Gender, Sex and Sexuality

Our gender identities are based on expectations placed on us by society – these are the 'rules' I mentioned earlier. Some of us break free of these, but we are still kept in line by them. The rules other people expect us to stick to suggest how we should behave. These rules can give other people the wrong idea about us, about who we are!

Our sex – or body parts – part of the body lottery – is not something we're in control of. However, these body parts are one of the few ways the world sees us as individuals. Our body parts are not really involved in who we are as people. Yet it is these body parts that give the world rules to stick to. So our sex can affect how others see our gender, which is then used to assume our sexuality.

It is actually quite confusing when you stop to explore the link between gender, sex and sexuality! My head is spinning and I have been talking about this for years! So it is okay if you don't fully understand this yet.

Why Do We Have Gender, Sex and Sexuality Then?

Most of this book is going to be positive. However, some parts will not be as nice. This is because some bits of life are not so great. In order to enjoy the good parts, we have to understand the less good bits.

Without the pressure of these rules, we are wonderful balls of potential. This means we can all decide who we are, and what matters to us. This includes how we form families, the jobs we have, and so many other things. This scares some people, like the rule makers, because this goes against what people have done in the past – or what is expected. Gender roles, linked to sex and affecting sexualities, are used to put us into categories. These categories are used by our government – the rule makers – and other big organizations to make money.

This sounds quite unpleasant, and if you look too closely, it is! However, this is a simple fact of life – people have to be useful. We can all define what we think is useful, but there are people who are in charge who make decisions for us. Our gender, sex and sexuality all play into where we end up in society – thanks to the 'rule' makers.

Hegemony and Heteronormativity

Hegemony – pronounced hej-e-mon-ee – is a set of rules that keeps things the same in society. Think about the rules that you stick by, to keep the grown-ups in your life happy. These are the rules that inform all the choices you make. Hegemony is a set of rules based on values the people in charge think benefit society. This can be political – like having taxes that benefit the wealthiest people – or this can be people-centred – like favouring white people over Black, Indigenous and people of colour (BIPOC).

We all know children at school who are 'popular' – they get to choose what is cool and what isn't cool. This is a form of hegemony.

Hegemony uses other social behaviours to police these rules. This is heteronormativity. We have seen the start of this word when we learned about sexualities – heterosexual. Heteronormativity is the idea that heterosexual people and behaviours are the most 'normal' thing. Heteronormativity likes the idea that girls who like boys and boys who like girls are better than people who are different.

An example of heteronormative behaviour is asking a girl what her dream husband would be like. To assume a girl is heterosexual suggests that the question asker thinks this is the most 'normal' option. We all know that there are lots of different genders and sexualities. We also know that lots of girls don't want husbands or even want to get married. This is how silly heteronormative behaviour is!

Hegemony and heteronormativity are best friends. Their relationship is totally toxic. Their behaviour is one of the main reasons why there is less support for LGBTQIA+ people. It has always been this way, and although things have changed, they are still doing a lot of damage together.

Stereotypes – They're Behind You!

If hegemony and heteronormativity are the villains in the pantomime about gender, stereotypes are the people who carry out their orders! Taken at face value, stereotypes are not that bad. They are something we all use when we meet people. Stereotypes are how we store information about people.

When we meet new people, we fill in a form in our brains. This form is full of simple questions. Questions like – what is this person's gender? Does this person like sport? Does this person have hair? This form and the answers we create goes on to become the set of information we hold on this person.

Ordering things in this way is our brain's way of keeping things simple. If we had to hold on to all the information about all the people we met, our heads would explode! So stereotypes are something we all use. They are only bad when we use the information gathered by our brains in a bad way. This is where someone uses an answer to judge a person.

An example of this would be someone assuming a boy who is gay doesn't like sport. The stereotype here is that sport is only for heterosexual boys, and that homosexual boys are not as masculine. This is very damaging behaviour. Using stereotypes like this causes harm to lots of people, and can result in very difficult relationships with other people and the wider world.

What Gender, Sex and Sexuality Mean for You

The big thing that you need to take from all of the words you have just read is that *you* are in charge. It can be tricky talking about our gender, sex and sexuality. This is even harder because so many of the things we think about when we have these discussions are thoughts from others. It would be amazing if the things we thought about ourselves were just based on our *own thoughts*. Sadly, this is not how the world works.

It can be very confusing to get to know yourself when you are dealing with hegemony and heteronormativity swirling around you. Some days will be easier than others, but some may be tough. The most important thing is that you are always kind to yourself. You also need to know that so many other people will feel similar things to you too. This is not a struggle you're going through alone.

Role Model: Lizzo (she/her)

Lizzo is a magical person. She is a singer, rapper and songwriter, and plays the flute. She comes from Detroit, Michigan in the USA. She is a body positivity icon, and has shown people all over the world that you are incredible, whatever your size and shape.

Lizzo is also a huge advocate for the LGBTQIA+ community. She has never specifically used the term 'pansexual' to describe her sexuality, but has suggested this in interviews.

'When it comes to sexuality or gender, I personally don't ascribe to just one thing. I cannot sit here right now and tell you I'm just one thing,' she said to *Teen Vogue*. 'That's why the colours for LGBTQ+ are a rainbow! Because there's a spectrum, and right now we try to keep it black and white. That's just not working for me.'[1]

Lizzo is a wonderful role model, showing you how to be confident in your own skin, and owning the thing that makes *you* unique.

Key Takeaways from this Chapter

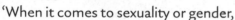

- ♥ Gender is confusing, and that's okay.
- ♥ Gender, sex and sexuality are all different – but they also overlap.
- ♥ Gender is how you feel.
- ♥ Sex is about your body parts.
- ♥ Sexuality is who you like.
- ♥ Ainsley Harriott is a lovely man!
- ♥ Hegemony and heteronormativity are toxic!
- ♥ Stereotypes are okay as long as they're not misused!
- ♥ You are in charge of your gender and sexuality – never forget this!

Gender, Sex and Sexuality Quiz

This chapter was heavy going – we have covered some very big subjects together. There are plenty of very powerful grown-ups who don't know half of the things that you have just read – so I wouldn't blame you if you feel a bit overwhelmed!

To help some of the key facts sink in a little better, I have created a mini quiz to see how much you can remember, and to show you what you might need to spend a little more time looking at again. Good luck!

1. Our gender is not about the physical body parts. What is our gender?
   a. Our pet rabbit
   b. The way we feel, as a person
   c. How other people treat us

2. When is our sex assigned?
   a. During Pride month
   b. On your 11th birthday
   c. At birth

3. What does your assigned sex not do?
   a. Define you
   b. Answer the phone
   c. Play the piano

4. What are the things in our society that make it harder for LGBTQIA+ people to be supported?
   a. Clowns
   b. Tap dancing
   c. Hegemony and heteronormativity

5. Who is in charge of your gender, sex and sexuality?
    a. Your teachers
    b. You
    c. Ainsley Harriott

Chapter 2

The Lion, the Witch and the Gender Identities in the Wardrobe

In the last chapter, we discussed how gender has become something of a big deal. Now we know that gender is different to sex and sexuality, we need to really delve into the world of gender. If you have read *The Lion, the Witch and the Wardrobe*, you will recall that Lucy first stumbles across Narnia through the wardrobe in the spare bedroom, all while the world was unaware that it existed.

Many people go about their lives oblivious of Narnia and the wonderful various gender identities out there. You and I are perhaps a bit more curious, so we are going to delve into the wardrobe of gender identities. There will be far fewer talking animals, no snow queen, and absolutely no selling out our siblings for Turkish delight! Instead we will gently uncover some of the magical ways people can explore and express their identity.

In this chapter we will:

- Explore the many ways that gender has been 'created'.
- Investigate the trans umbrella – and explore all that lies underneath.
- Look at what life is like without any particular gender.
- Oh, and, of course, we can't forget to say hello to Mr Tumnus!*

Gender Is a Social Construct

This might sound a little confusing, but don't you worry. Social construct simply means something that humans have created, and agree to being real, but in reality doesn't exist physically. An example of this is borders between countries.

* We won't actually have time to meet Mr Tumnus; for that you'll need a copy of *The Lion, the Witch and the Wardrobe*!

Borders exist on maps, but there are often no walls or fences. They only exist because rule makers say so!

This is what we mean when we say that gender is a social construct. So much of it has been created by culture and society. How can gender ever have been anything more than a set of 'rules' to be ignored or rewritten? Once you see gender for what it is – as just a set of guidelines – you realize that you get to make more decisions when it comes to your own gender.

So we are clear that there is a difference between gender and sex. Society is less clear on this difference. It uses binary sex, and places gender expectations on people. This means that some people – mainly those who make the rules, and shouty people on Twitter – think our bodies define our gender roles.

This is exactly the opposite of the truth – because gender is essentially a set of guidelines. Think of it like LEGO®. With the instructions that come in the box, you could build the set as it says. But if you threw those instructions away, you could build anything you wanted – there would be so many options you could build. This is what living beyond the gender binary is.

This is the fun bit. Gender is yours to shape. You get to make the rules for yourself; you're in charge!

The Trans Umbrella

When you begin to discover your own gender identity, you will become more aware of the word 'trans'. Trans, or transgender, is a term for anyone who doesn't identify with the gender they were assigned at birth. Transgender – the word – owes its structure to Greek. 'Trans' means 'beyond', 'across' or 'on the other side of'! So transgender means beyond gender and the 'rules' of society.

Trans is a nice and welcoming term that includes lots of people who feel they don't belong. Some trans people transition into their chosen gender – which means they can change from the sex they were assigned at birth to a sex or gender identity that feels comfortable to them.

However, not all trans people transition in a medical way (operations that change the way people's bodies look), some people will change their names, and some won't. The welcoming nature of the word 'trans' means that some people live without any gender at all. Trans has become a very accepting community of like-minded people who are making the decisions about their own gender without any rules.

What Not to Say!

As with all parts of life, the words we use to talk about things change as we learn more. This is part of the process of human evolution, the constant way we can all learn and be better people. When we talk about the trans umbrella, and the trans community as a whole, we are talking about transgender people.

Some people see the word 'trans' and think we are talking about the word 'transvestite'. Transvestite is a term that used to be used for people who wore clothes of the 'opposite gender'. This is a very outdated term, and most people in the community would not use this word at all.

Language is personal to us all. So some people within the trans community may use this word. However, most of us don't, and if you're outside of the trans community, I would steer clear of this word.

Cisgender! It's Not a Bad Word!

The conversation about trans people has become a lot bigger recently. TV and newspapers are kind of obsessed! One word that you may see being used in these conversations is 'cisgender' or 'cis'.

Cisgender describes anyone who identifies with the sex they were assigned at birth, typically meaning male or female. This means that anyone who is happy with the sex they were assigned at birth, and does not feel the need to question it, is cisgender.

Transgender as a word has a rich and varied history. Fast-forward to the 21st century, and it is the key way we describe the community. If the trans community has a label, then it makes sense for people outside of the community to have a label too. It means we can always accurately describe people, and this is why we use the word cisgender.

Cisgender people sometimes get a bit huffy about the use of this word, but this is silly. Cisgender is not a bad word; in fact, it is very helpful. So don't be afraid to use it!

Who Belongs Under the Trans Umbrella?

We have got ourselves comfortable with the idea that gender is something we're in charge of. The trans umbrella exists for people who want to explore, change and be in charge of their gender. Now is a good time to explore some of the different gender identities that sit under the trans umbrella.

Trans Men and Women

'Trans men and women' refers to people who are usually not comfortable with the sex they were assigned at birth. Trans men and women have either begun to socially transition or have medically transitioned. Just because someone is trans does not automatically mean they hate their body or identity. However, a trans person chooses to explore their gender, to better understand who they are, and their gender identity. Being trans is very important to them, and should be respected by all of us.

Living as the gender and/or sex they have chosen for themselves is the magical part of being trans. In society we see and hear more about trans women, but trans men are just as valid and special too, and when we talk about trans people we must make sure we are including *all trans people*.

Non-Binary

Gender is easy to imagine as colours. Male can be seen as blue and female as pink. Many people assume incorrectly that non-binary is purple – a blend of two gender identities – which is an easy mistake to make. Non-binary exists like a colour wheel, with 'typical assumed' male and female identifiers sitting in certain places. A non-binary person is any combination of colours on that wheel, up, down and all around.

Non-binary as a term is so wonderfully welcoming. It doesn't hold you back, or require anyone to be at a fixed point on that colour wheel. It can be confusing to wrap your head around this if you are new to this subject, especially when many of us have grown up in a world fixed by binary 'rules' of gender, but it is simple. Non-binary is not fixed and has no rules. Not all non-binary people will identify as trans, and some will – this is a personal approach – but non-binary people are very much welcome under the trans umbrella.

Gender-Fluid and Genderqueer

Genderqueer is a term for those who don't feel comfortable among gender binaries and norms. Instead they choose to mix gender identities. This means they are in complete control of their gender identity.

Similar to non-binary people, gender-fluid and genderqueer people are all unique. This means each person will define their identity in slightly different ways. This is what makes gender exciting – because we are in charge – and it means we can truly be who we are!

Two-Spirit

Two-Spirit is an umbrella term (like trans) that bridges the gap between Indigenous (an example of Indigenous people are Native Americans, who were living in America before the European settlers) and western approaches to gender and sexuality. Different groups have different definitions, but most agree this is another gender option, beyond female and male.

It is a relatively fresh term used in popular culture. However, Two-Spirit has been used by Indigenous groups for centuries. It was offered by non-western teaching as a way of honouring tradition as well as preserving heritage and non-western beliefs.

Agender

The 'a' here means 'without' or 'none'. So agender people are without gender, and express that, however they want. This can be similar to non-binary, gender-fluid and genderqueer people. There are similarities, that's for sure.

Whether you think something is similar or not, the language people choose to use to describe themselves is very important – carry on reading to find out more about respect.

Respecting Gender Identities

Respect is an interesting word, and what it means is having care for someone else. Respecting how people choose to define their gender identity is very important. Knowing that many people take time to figure out their gender identity means we owe them complete respect for that journey.

It can be hard, because we can be led by our own understanding of terms and identities. However, the way someone else chooses to identify is as they say it is and is not up for debate. I am sure this is how you would like to be treated, so it makes sense to offer this branch of courtesy to others too!

Role Model: Ki Griffin (he/they)

The wonderful Ki Griffin is an actor and campaigner. They were the first non-binary and intersex actor to become a regular cast member in Channel 4's soap *Hollyoaks*:

> I do hope that my role can inspire other young people who didn't feel there was a place in the performance industries for them, even if they didn't feel there was a place in the world for them, to live freely and authentically as themselves. I want them to see me and know they are enough, no matter who they are.[2]

Ki is an amazing person to look up to, as they are a trailblazer, making waves in the acting world and creating real moments of real representation, on and off screen!

Key Takeaways from this Chapter

- ♥ Gender identities are a big thing – and it's okay to be overwhelmed.
- ♥ Gender is made up – so you only need to please yourself!
- ♥ Trans is an inclusive and accepting word, and a community of like-minded people.
- ♥ There are lots of ways to be trans – they are all real.
- ♥ Trans men are very real!
- ♥ Non-binary is hard to define – and that is the whole point – there is no one definition for non-binary!
- ♥ People have existed outside of binary gender for centuries – like Two-Spirit people.
- ♥ Agender is just people living without gender – very simple!
- ♥ However anyone identifies, we respect that.

Gender Identities Crossword

Wow! I feel like we learned loads from this chapter. Certainly I think it might take time for all of the terms to become second nature. So I thought a crossword might be a great way to try out the things you have just learned.

Use the descriptions below to figure out which term or word fits. It's okay if you need to flip back over the last few pages to help you answer them – you're still learning! Have fun...

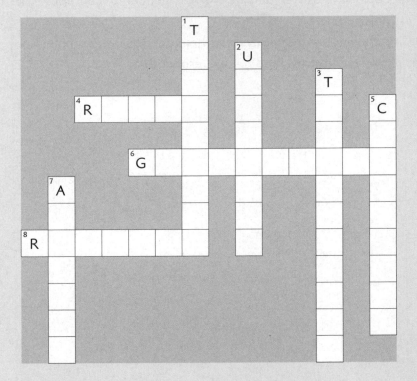

Across

4. Non-binary is not fixed and has no...
6. Gender is a set of...
8. Having care for someone else is...

Down

1. Bridges the gap between Indigenous and western approaches to gender and sexuality (3-6).

2. Transgender is an...term.
3. Anyone who doesn't identify with the gender they were assigned at birth.
5. Anyone who identifies with the sex they were assigned at birth.
7. People who are without gender can identify as...

Chapter 3

Pronouns Aren't People

Normally when you start a chapter with me, we have a little introduction. However, for this to make sense we need to have a definition first.

What Is a Pronoun?

Pronouns are how we describe ourselves. They are also the way we refer to other people. In a sentence we would say:

'Janet had a long day; *she* is tired' – *she* is the pronoun in this sentence.

We could also say:

'Sasha talks all the time; *they* are very talkative!' – *they* is the pronoun in this sentence.

If this was an English lesson – it isn't, don't worry – it would be explained to you in a different way. Your teacher would say something like: a pronoun is a substitute for a noun (names) or a noun phrase. Where we would use a name we can also use a pronoun.

Pronouns are split into singular and plural (more than one) versions:

Talking about yourself: I, me, my, mine, myself.
Talking about yourself and someone else: we, us, our, ours, ourselves.
Talking about someone else: you, your, yours, yourself.
Talking about multiple people: you, your, yours, yourselves.

Talking about a girl: she, her, hers, herself.

Talking about a boy: he, him, his, himself.

Talking about a genderless person: they, them, their, theirs, themself or themselves.

This might seem very complicated. But now you know what pronouns are and their role in language. This is a great place to start this chapter!

In this chapter we will:

- Explore why pronouns have become such a big deal.
- Investigate the history of pronouns.
- Look at the arguments people use to suggest neutral pronouns are 'bad' or 'wrong'.
- Oh, and, of course, we can't forget about making mistakes!

Why Are We Talking about Pronouns?

When I was growing up, I don't remember there being a big conversation about pronouns. I don't even remember being taught them at school! Pronouns have been used in language since language began. Pronouns are something that just happen, like rain, or getting hungry. So they are nothing new!

The last couple of years have seen a big focus on pronouns. People, businesses and the media are all more aware of the LGBTQIA+ community. This new awareness is also throwing more attention on to transgender people, and gender-diverse people. Some people use gender-neutral pronouns: they, them, theirs. This can feel new and scary the first time people see this.

Pronouns have become something of a debate across the world. Politicians, newspapers, TV and so many others have all had something to say about people who use 'they' or 'them'. These angry people always say that using 'they' or 'them' is new, scary or confusing – or something like that! There are plenty of reasons people think like this. I will let you into a secret – they're all wrong!

Keep reading to learn all about pronouns and why the angry people are just being silly!

Gender-Neutral Pronouns 101

I have already introduced the idea of gender-neutral pronouns to you. This is people who use 'they', 'them', 'theirs' as the way to describe themselves. This has become a very popular way for non-binary people, trans people and genderqueer people to refer to themselves.

It might surprise you to know that there are lots of other gender-neutral pronouns in use too! Here are some common and some less common gender-neutral pronouns used today:

- They, them, their, theirs, themself
- Zie, zim, zir, zis, zieself
- Sie, sie, hir, hirs, hirself
- Ey, em, eir, eirs, eirself
- Ve, ver, vis, versl, verself
- Tey, ter, tem, ters, terself
- E, em, eir, eirs, emself
- Xe, xem, xyr, xyrs, xemself
- Fae, fae, faer, faers, faerself
- Per, per, pers, pers, perself.

It is clear that there are a lot of different options out there for you to try. If you want to use gender-neutral pronouns, then I recommend you try them out, and see how you feel. Just like buying shoes, it can take a little while to find the ones that fit you just right. There is no rush when it comes to picking your pronouns. I use 'they/them' pronouns, and to begin with I wasn't sure, but now they feel so comfy!

They/She, They/He and They/She/He

There are also people who use 'they' and non-neutral pronouns. This can look like 'he/they', 'she/they' or 'they/she/he'.

The reasons people have for their pronouns are always personal to them. A person who uses 'they/she' may identify as a woman and non-binary – so they have both pronouns. The one they use first – in this case, 'they' – is the one they prefer, but they are okay being referred to as 'she' too. It is another layer of the pronoun cake!

When you come across a set of pronouns you have not seen before – whether it is 'xe/xem', 'they/them' or 'she/they' – the best thing to do is ask. Politely ask that person how they wish to be referred to, and then you can tell them your pronouns too. Doing this is respectful, and makes new interactions more inclusive (including all people, regardless of gender, sex or sexuality) for everyone!

It's All History!

The oldest gender-neutral pronoun in the English language is singular 'they'. This was used happily for centuries to describe anyone and everyone, and if you didn't know their gender – how polite! If you look in the dictionary, the exact date we have written evidence of singular 'they' can be pinpointed – all the way back to 1375!

It appears in the medieval romance *William and the Werewolf*, also known as *William of Palerne*, written in around 1200 (dates can get wobbly in history!).

It was translated from French into Middle English in 1375. The Middle English looks like this: 'Hastely hiȝed eche…þei neyȝþed so neiȝh…þere william & his worþi lef were liand i-fere.' Are you still following me?!

Don't worry, we have the modern equivalent of this here: 'Each man hurried…till *they* drew near…where William and his darling were lying together.' The sentence refers to singular men as *they*. This is concrete evidence of 'they' being used to refer to singular people. Now this is just the first written example; it will have been used in speech long before that – which means singular 'they' may well be far older than we thought.

In 1996, the former chief editor of the *Oxford English Dictionary*, Robert Burchfield, made it clear how he saw this conversation. He said that people were happy to use 'they/them' in both singular and plural ways. The objections that people have are not sensible:

> People who want to be inclusive, or respectful of other people's preferences, use singular they. And people who don't want to be inclusive, or who don't respect other people's pronoun choices, use singular they as well. Even people who object to singular they as a grammatical error use it themselves when they're not looking.[3]

What Robert is saying is that everyone uses 'they/them' in lots of different ways. The point here is that we all use it. So the argument that it is all so new and scary is clearly not correct!

The Grammar Police

The next argument people use is that using 'they/them' to refer to a single person is 'grammatically incorrect'. If I made a pound for every time I heard this, I could buy everyone reading this book an ice cream! This argument is really very silly for a few reasons.

They can be used to refer to multiple people (plural) but we also use *they* and *them* to refer to single people all the time. Seriously, we do!

> James went to the supermarket. *They* were ages.
> Suzy is so messy. I will have to clear up after *them* again.

These are simple little sentences that remind us that we all use 'they' and 'them' to refer to single people.

Misgendering and Mistakes

Misgendering is where someone is referred to by the wrong pronoun. This is something that happens from time to time. It isn't the end of the world, but it can feel very strange. When someone misgenders you, it feels like they aren't talking about *you* any more.

The first time someone misgenders a person it is a mistake. This is okay. If that person goes on to repeatedly misgender, refusing to learn, then this is not okay. People can carry on misgendering someone even though they know it is not right. This is because 'he' and 'she' is their natural response. How they deal with this mistake will show you whether they can learn or not.

Knowing how to deal with these mistakes is very important.

When people get pronouns wrong, sometimes they make it into a very big deal. This is not the way to approach this. I always advise people to simply apologize and move on. For example:

> Incorrect person: 'Have you asked him if he wants a cup of tea?'
>
> Corrector: 'Have you asked *them* if *they* want a cup of tea?'
>
> Incorrect person: '*Them*, yes, apologies! Have you asked *them* if *they* want a cup of tea?'

This is a very simple yet effective way to make sure the mistake stays small. When people make a fuss, it can actually make gender-diverse people feel very uneasy. This makes us feel like we have to make sure the incorrect person's feelings are not hurt. But if we keep this conversation small, it doesn't get blown out of proportion. So if anyone asks you how to deal with pronoun mistakes, now you know!

Practice Makes Perfect

It can be tricky when someone changes their pronouns, or if this is the first person you have met who uses neutral pronouns. However, the more we try, the easier it becomes. The first time you rode a bike I am sure you might have fallen off, but you got better with time. So practice makes perfect.

One question I get asked a lot is 'What do I do if I really cannot get my head around pronouns?' We can only know what we know. If we don't know something, how are we expected to fully understand it? This is why some people get angry about new things, because they don't fully understand it, and it makes them nervous.

When it comes to pronouns, there is a conversation about doing things 'right' and 'wrong'. For those who can't get it, it can feel like they're a 'bad person'. This causes them to run away from the conversation. This is much worse than getting a pronoun wrong! It is key that people remember they need to learn! By finding things hard, and getting it wrong, you're just showing that you are human and you can learn.

The best thing to do with this feeling of confusion is to see it as a chance to learn. This will make sure that we are all doing our best – which is all anyone can ask.

I do have a very simple way to get round the 'pronoun' issue. Simply use a person's name, every time you refer to them. You will be doing it in the most respectful manner possible. So until you get comfortable with gender-neutral pronouns, this is an easy way around it.

All Is Not What You See!

One element that can make misgendering an issue is 'passing'. Passing is a term we use when someone appears to belong to a social group that they actually don't. This can be used to describe race, gender, sexuality and disability. In terms of gender and pronouns, passing means that someone assumes a person's gender purely based on the way they look. This means they could very easily misgender someone.

Human brains are very complex, but also at their core they are very simple indeed. We truly believe that seeing is believing – how could our brains ever lie to us? Our brains can see a person, hear them tell us their pronouns, and their gender identity, and still refer to them incorrectly. It may feel very hard, and your brain may have very strong feelings about this.

Regardless of how someone looks, we always have to respect the pronouns the person uses.

The easiest thing to remember is that everyone is unique. We should treat everyone with respect. This means that what someone says is more valid than how we think they look. Remember this the next time you see it happening, or if your brain tries to trick you!

Role Model: Indya Moore (they/she)

Indya Moore is an incredible person. They are an actor and model. They are best known for playing Angel in a TV show called *Pose*. Indya is transgender and non-binary and uses they/she pronouns. They have created so much visibility for our community by working with fashion brands such as Louis Vuitton, and have even attended the Met Gala in New York.

They are not always comfortable being called a role model. They told *Dazed* that:

I'm honoured to be that for other people, but

I'm also a work in progress. I don't ever want anyone to outline their life after mine. I'm not perfect, I'm very flawed; the ways that I love are very complicated. I always want people to see the best parts of themselves in me. I'm very happy to be that reflection, wherever I can be. Even when people see themselves in the places (in me) that are dark, that's also helpful. It's human to have shortcomings. There's space for transparency in all that.[4]

Indya is a great person to take inspiration from, because they show us that life is about small daily change – and that is very powerful.

Key Takeaways from this Chapter

- ♥ A pronoun is how we describe ourselves.
- ♥ Pronouns can be confusing, and that's okay.
- ♥ Pronouns are different for different people – it's a personal choice.
- ♥ It's respectful to ask people their pronouns.
- ♥ There is a lot of history behind pronouns – so ignore the shouty people!
- ♥ You will know when your pronouns feel right for you!
- ♥ If it is hard at first, simply use a person's name!
- ♥ Practice makes perfect!
- ♥ We should treat everyone with respect.

Pronoun Bingo

To chart your progress with pronouns through this chapter, it's time to play a game! All you need to do is cross off the squares as you understand pronouns, and begin to work this understanding into your life. The first with a full house (all boxes crossed) wins. Dabbers at the ready...

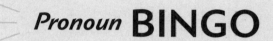

Pronoun **BINGO**

You know that pronouns are how we refer to ourselves or others.	You know that the big conversation around pronouns is very silly!	You know that there are lots more options than she/her, they/them and he/him.
Regardless of how someone looks, you know to always respect the pronouns they use.	*Pronoun Bingo*	Ignore the grumpy shouty people – using they/them is not grammatically incorrect!
You know it can take time to feel comfortable with new pronouns.	You have ways to ensure you quickly overcome mistakes – and are trying your best when it comes to pronouns.	You know that practice makes perfect!

Chapter 4
Question Time

imagine one of the reasons you picked up this book is to answer some of the burning questions you may have about yourself. This is a very good reason to read this book, and I am thrilled you have chosen it to help! This is the chapter where we talk about them. We will also try to make these conversations easier.

I can't read your mind – it would be weird if I could – so I might not talk directly about one of your questions. However, we will cover some of the main conversations you may be having or want to find out about your gender identity. There will be some more detailed solutions and suggestions in the chapters following on from this one. However, we had better stick to the chapter at hand for now.

In this chapter we will:

- Explore why the questions you may have seem so big.
- Get to grips with other people.
- Talk about a pink poodle named Sharon.
- Oh, and, of course, we can't forget about looking at these questions a different way!

Big Questions

Before we tackle the 'why's, we need to first address the 'what's, 'how's and 'who's – a silly sentence, but a valid one. I want to help you tackle feeling unsure, and I also want to then look at the things that can help you. However, as I mentioned, we first need to explore the 'Big Questions' you may have, and what they could mean.

When we call these questions 'Big Questions' it makes me feel like they are huge towering trees looking down on me. This isn't that helpful, because, in reality, how we look at things changes their size. On the ground trees are very tall. However, if you see things from the sky looking down, such as from a helicopter, suddenly the very tall trees seem very small. This is called perspective.

This means that at first the questions we have in our minds may feel big, but with the perspective of knowledge (which you will find in these pages), suddenly they are no longer towering over you. Perspective is so helpful.

Who Do You Want to Be When You Grow Up?

When I was growing up, the main question we were asked was, 'What do you want to be when you grow up?' Now my answer at four years old was – of course – a lady truck driver. Sadly, I can say that has yet to happen, but if you know someone who drives a truck, do send them my way! However, looking back I can see that this question wasn't very helpful, yet it was one of the bigger focus points of conversation at school.

I think a much more important question is, *'Who do you want to be when you grow up?'* I don't ever recall being asked this question. Who we want to be is more important than what we might do. The 'who' trumps the 'what'! This is a much more important part of our lives, and deserves much more thinking time. Don't worry, I am not expecting you to have an answer right now, or even ever. It can be a constant work in progress!

Thinking about who you want to be, and the relationship that has with where you are right now, takes time. It might be one of the reasons that led you to pick up this book. Reading the pages of this book is a good place to ponder who you want to be.

A Note on Other People

The writer Jean-Paul Sartre famously once wrote that 'Hell is other people'. This is often quoted in books and TV. Some people find this to be true, and others don't. I don't always look on the bright side, but I do think this quote has some lessons we can learn from. As with all quotes, there is room for us all to take different meanings from it. From my point of view, I see that other people have lots of opinions. The opinions can be very personal, and make LGBTQIA+ community members feel very uncomfortable.

These opinions will probably be part of the worries you may have. This uncomfortable ability other people have to make us feel less great is why I refer to 'Hell is other people'. The best way through this is by remembering that it is not your job to agree with everyone, or even to try to make them comfortable. Your one and only job is to make yourself comfortable.

You will meet lovely people along the way, too, but all it takes is one bad situation to make you doubt yourself. Remember — doing what is right for you is always the right decision.

Sharon, the Pink Poodle

On my desk there is a money box in the shape of a pink poodle. She is named 'Sharon'. She was a gift, which I chose myself. My family couldn't understand why I would choose something they consider to be very poor taste. The silly thing is, even today, I can't form a sentence to explain why I love Sharon so much — I just do. When we choose something others see as different, they will question you about it, making you uncomfortable.

This can happen for things like Sharon, but it can also be for things like our gender. You might not have all the words for how you feel, but you know you feel something, that this is completely accurate. You may never have all the words to describe and prove how you feel, and that doesn't matter. You are still the same person; you still like the same things, and enjoy life. The most important thing is that you know what you do and do not want for yourself.

People may question you throughout your life, but it is not your job to defend yourself. Your job is to be yourself, and to enjoy your life. People crave answers for the unknown, but you don't have to give them any. Life isn't *Mastermind*! So it is okay to be just like Sharon; be fabulous and don't be tied down by others' feelings!

Girl, Boy, Other?

In Chapter 2 we explored gender identities together, diving into all the options that are out there. Among them, we probably didn't pay much attention to cisgender people. Cisgender people identify with the sex they were assigned at birth. You might feel like this too, and that is great.

You might be reading this book because you don't feel like a girl or a boy, or you may feel like a boy, but people around you think that you're a girl. The first thing to say is this is all very much part of being human. Just because many of the people around you may not be coming up with the same questions doesn't mean you're wrong. Questioning your gender is okay. It has also been done for thousands of years.

Questioning your gender identity is nothing new. It may feel like a big deal right now, but I promise you, it isn't that huge. I talked earlier about perspective. This is something we can use to help this question feel much more comfortable.

I Don't Want to Disappoint My Family

We talked earlier about the idea that 'Hell is other people'. However, our families aren't just anyone. They're important to us. These are the people who have been there for us since day one. It can feel like a huge deal to share a side of yourself they might not know about. It can feel scary when you don't know how they will react. It can be difficult when you have to juggle this worry alongside all the others you may have.

I don't know how your family will respond. Some grown-ups or brothers and sisters may know you better than you think, and are just waiting to have that conversation with you and put you at ease. Some family members may be surprised, but not worried by what you share with them. Some family members may take a lot longer to adjust to what you tell them. There is no hard and fast rule to this kind of conversation.

The most important thing I can share with you is that your happiness is just as important as your family's happiness. Working out who you are and what you want from your life is not a bad thing. Families can be difficult and wonderful all at the same time. It is helpful to have someone to talk to, and I will share some information about this in Chapter 6, 'Feeling Lonely? Read This!'

What If I Change My Mind?

Changing your mind is a big topic, and one the media likes to talk about the most. We can ignore the press, because they don't have a say about how any of us feel right here. This is a safe space, and it is a good question to ask. Changing your mind sounds like a 'yes' or 'no' kind of idea, doesn't it? Well, you won't decide that you are non-binary tomorrow and then, in three years, wake up and say, 'Nope, I am a cisgender girl'. Things are not that black and white!

Changing your mind is about the constant way people change. As things become clearer to us, so does our understanding of ourselves. This is a constant process that everyone goes through, and not just LGBTQIA+ people. So don't worry about what might happen in the future. Just be happy with the choices you are making for yourself right now. This is the best way to approach any of these questions.

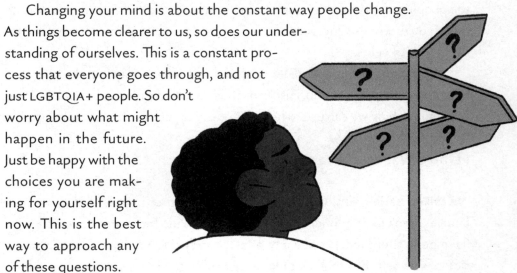

Let's Look at the Questions a Different Way!

When we question our gender, the people around us begin to have questions of their own. These gender questions are what might make your gender identity feel like a big deal. Remembering that these are questions from other people, and not yourself, is important.

I said we would use perspective to show you it isn't a big deal. I thought we could answer some of the gender questions together. All we will use is what you have already read in the book so far.

Q: I only believe in boys and girls – how can you not identify as one of those?

A: Gender is a social idea that has such importance because people make it so, like borders. You need to forget how you think people should identify. Everyone is in charge of their own identity, and while you might not identify that way, you cannot stop anyone else being themselves!

Q: You don't look like a girl – why not?

A: Gender is how we feel, not how we look. How you think a girl should look is because of stereotypes. We need to give people the space to do things for themselves. How someone looks does not change their gender identity.

Q: If you can be non-binary, why can't I identify as a penguin?

A: I am not choosing my gender out of thin air. I don't feel comfortable with binary gender options of 'girl' and 'boy' to define myself. This doesn't mean I am not human! By asking about identifying as a penguin, you're making it into something very different. I am still human, as are you, so no, you can't identify as a penguin!

Q: I know another trans person – why aren't you like them?

A: No two humans are the same. Just because we're both trans doesn't mean we're the same person. Being trans is not a personality or a look. It is an important gender identity, and allows me to be the person I truly am. I do not have to act or look a certain way!

I have answered some of the more technical questions for you. I have also left a couple blank for you to answer yourself, because I know you can do this!

Q: How do you know your gender identity is not the same any more?

. . . .

Q: Your personality is the same! Why hasn't that changed?

. . . .

Role Model: Marsha P. Johnson (she/her)

Marsha P. Johnson fought for many of the rights we have today. She was part of the uprising at the Stonewall riots of 1969, where police targeted an LGBTQIA+ bar called the Stonewall Inn. The people in the bar decided enough was enough and fought back against the police. This led to days of rioting, which sparked the Pride movement we now know and love. Lots of people credit Marsha with being the person who threw the first brick during these riots, which she always denied. She was also part of an activist group, known as Act Up, which fought for the rights of those who had the virus known as HIV/Aids.

Marsha lived her life to create change for the community, and the wider world: 'How many years has it taken people to realize that we are all brothers and sisters and human beings in the human race?'[5]

Marsha sadly died in 1992, but her efforts to change things have lived on for generations. We will always be grateful for all that Marsha P. Johnson achieved and made possible for us.

Key Takeaways from this Chapter

- ♥ With perspective, big questions don't feel so big.
- ♥ Thinking about who you want to be is a good place to start.
- ♥ Other people can be difficult – this is not your fault.
- ♥ Making sure you're happy is a good thing!
- ♥ You might not have all the words for how you feel, and that's okay.
- ♥ Questioning your gender identity is nothing new! It's been happening for centuries.
- ♥ Families can be difficult and wonderful all at the same time.
- ♥ Nothing is set in stone, so get ready to change over time.
- ♥ Other people may question you, but you should never doubt yourself!

Question Time Word Search

This chapter has a lot you might want to reflect on. This is something that you need to make some time for, and so, to help you do that, why not give the Question Time Word Search a go — simply cross the words out as you find them — there are ten in total.

```
R  N  R  Y  E  R  E  L  W  D  B  F  I  G  P
G  W  C  B  Y  M  B  L  N  Y  E  Z  N  T  E
M  M  A  P  C  O  O  D  D  E  W  I  N  L  R
S  C  T  Z  D  H  E  T  L  O  N  P  X  U  S
Z  F  R  W  L  J  B  T  I  O  O  N  E  C  P
C  H  A  N  G  E  J  V  I  O  T  P  Z  I  E
S  Z  M  L  Z  L  L  T  G  W  N  V  K  F  C
T  L  N  S  M  O  S  T  X  R  B  S  A  F  T
O  B  L  L  K  E  S  J  K  E  T  M  K  I  I
B  S  D  F  U  N  X  J  B  D  A  Q  P  D  V
B  U  Q  Q  N  J  Q  Z  R  N  H  C  J  R  E
S  S  E  N  I  P  P  A  H  E  P  E  V  Z  Z
X  B  H  Y  T  F  N  D  N  G  U  N  O  Z  W
B  F  B  G  S  N  O  I  T  S  E  U  Q  H  P
Y  F  A  X  B  F  T  E  A  T  Z  F  K  P  B
```

QUESTIONS POODLE GENDER
QUESTIONING CHANGE
EMOTIONS PERSPECTIVE FEEL
HAPPINESS DIFFICULT

Chapter 5

I'm Not Sure, and That's Okay!

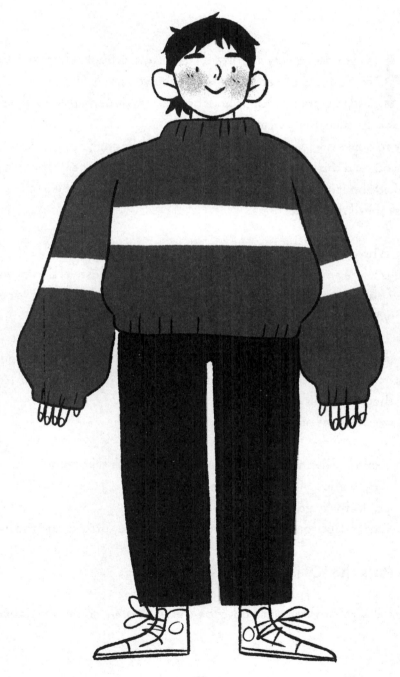

How you feel is very important to me, as this book is here to help you. The business of getting to know who you are is *huge*. It can be very hard to work this out on your own. So this is perhaps why you picked this book up, to learn more about yourself.

We're obviously talking about gender, and exploring your gender identity. So as you read this chapter I want you to think about some of the questions we talked about in the last chapter. Or you could maybe make it a little simpler and ask these three questions:

- Who do you want to be?
- Is there anything stopping you from being this best version of you?
- What three things would you change to become the best version of you?

These are pretty big questions that even adults struggle to answer. So you don't need to have answers right away, or even at all – but it will be helpful to think about them over this chapter.

As well as these questions, in this chapter we will:

- Explore why the process of becoming yourself takes time.
- Get to grips with already being perfect.
- Look at why good things take time.
- Oh, and, of course, we can't forget about the tortoise and the hare!

Who Puts the 'Q' in LGBTQIA+?

In the full acronym we use to describe the LGBTQIA+ community, there are two 'Q's. The first is 'queer', which is an open term used by many LGBTQIA+ people. The second is 'questioning'. Questioning means a person who is figuring out their gender identity, or sexual identity.

'Questioning' is a lovely way to describe yourself if you haven't fully worked out your gender identity. Anybody can be questioning, and if you talk to anyone in the LGBTQIA+ community, we have all been questioning at one point or another.

Some people work things out and stay there. Some people feel like they can adapt and change all the time, and keep things fluid. Other people pick an identity that gives them room to grow into themselves at their own pace – like genderqueer or non-binary.

However you look at it, being questioning is an inevitable part of growing up. Not knowing is not a bad thing! There is also no time limit, expectation or finishing line. You deserve all the time in the world to work out who you are, so take it!

You're Already Perfect

In this chapter, we are discussing the theme of change. This might be a change in gender identities and the language you use to talk about yourself. It could be a change in who you thought you were attracted to. Whatever that change might be, I don't want to take away from a very important fact:

You are perfect as you are right now.

Even if you have questions about how you might change, or a desire to understand some of the questions going around in your head, it doesn't stop you being a wonderful human being, head to toe!

It can be very easy to pick fault with your current state or level of knowledge. However, this is still a part of you. Basically, this version of you will always be part of you. If we wrote a story of your life, we would need to include who you are right now – it is very important! So please, never forget that you, yes you, are perfect right now.

Evolution – It's Human Nature

I didn't always pay too much attention at school, which, by the way, is not a good thing! This means that I have some gaps in my knowledge about things. However, one thing that always stuck was evolution. Evolution is the way living things change and develop over generations. Humans as we know them now have been on Earth for around the last two hundred thousand to three hundred thousand years.

We evolved from our closest ancestor *Homo erectus* – which means 'upright man' in Latin. However, human-like ancestors had been walking upright for almost five million years. There is evidence of our ancestors creating some stone tools as far back as two million years ago.

Science tells us that evolution happens over thousands of years, and for some characteristics this is true. For us as individuals, our understanding of ourselves evolves day after day. This happens as we grow and learn more about who we are.

The idea that we are fixed as we are is silly. We change every time we find out something new about ourselves. This doesn't mean huge shifts on a daily basis. Instead, over a couple of months, you may feel that things like gender and sexuality shift. It might not happen right now, but it may in the future.

Understanding that we all evolve as people can provide hope. This makes us all feel better, because as we change, we get a bigger sense of who we are. This makes it easier to form opinions, make decisions and find our purpose. Evolution is pretty amazing!

Life Isn't a Pressure Cooker

Grown-ups in certain professions like 'motivational speakers' throw around some pretty naff phrases. One of them is 'Diamonds are formed under pressure'. This is used to suggest that pressure – or tricky situations – helps create better people.

What they forget to mention is that same pressure can cause diamonds to explode when jewellers come to cut them for jewellery! So the whole pressure/diamond message is a complicated one. It is not always the helpful message some people think it is.

Pressure can be helpful. Steaming vegetables in a pressure cooker makes them tender and delicious. But we are not vegetables, *so we don't need pressure!*

Whether you think about vegetables or diamonds, you don't need to be under pressure to make the right decision when it comes to your gender or sexuality. Which very neatly brings me on to my next point.

Good Things Take Time

Another phrase said by adults is 'Good things take time'. Which means 'have patience', as some of the best things can't happen overnight. I like this, actually, because it is genuinely helpful. We live in a very fast-paced world where seemingly things happen at the tap of a finger on a screen.

Yet some things take a little while longer. This could be building a house, growing vegetables, or working out who you are as a person. These are all things that are worth waiting for. They are also worth spending time on as a project or a personal pursuit.

Sometimes we all wish things would move a little quicker. Are we there yet? How many days is it until Christmas? There is a fine line between anticipation and wishing your life away. It might feel like an age and that time is dragging. But when it comes to figuring yourself out, it is all about letting it take its time.

It's Not Just You

Growing up 'different' is hard. Difference is part of what makes people magical. Yet some people see difference as a threat. When we don't meet the grade to blend in with the rest of the world, we can feel really alone.

It is not uncommon to feel like this. It isn't fair, but it doesn't have to rule how you feel. I can say this with utter confidence – you are not alone in the way you feel. The reason I have popped in role models throughout this book is so you can see some amazing LGBTQIA+ community members. If you look at any of these amazing, creative, inspiring individuals, you will find that they, too, probably grew up feeling alone or 'different'.

Sadly, it might not make how you feel right now any better. However, knowing that it isn't just you can act as a comfort to you. You are wonderful. You're on the right path. You're not alone.

The Tortoise and the Hare

We can all dream of snapping our fingers and having all our problems fixed. Annoyingly, no one has worked out how to make this happen yet – fingers crossed for the future! However, here, in the real world, we have to do things a little bit slower – which isn't bad at all! Slow is good. Seriously, rushing things never gets good results!

We often hear the phrase 'Slow and steady wins the race'. This comes from a fable, *The Tortoise and the Hare*. In this story the tortoise challenges the hare to a race. The hare accepts, thinking it an easy challenge as tortoises are slow and hares are quick – a no-brainer, right? Well, the hare rushes off the start line, and confidently thinks he'll win, so stops for a nap. The hare wakes to find the tortoise crossing the finish line, winning the race.

The meaning is easy to see – slower approaches provide better results. Your life isn't a race to be won, but it does need time for it to develop nicely. So there is no need to rush!

Role Model: Billy Porter (he/him)

Billy Porter is a global superstar, and American actor, singer and writer. He first found fame on Broadway, and won a Tony award for his role of Lola in *Kinky Boots*. The world truly fell in love with Billy Porter after his critically acclaimed role of Pray Tell in the TV show *Pose*. He has gone on to win countless awards.

Porter is a champion of diversity and the unique nature of being part of the LGBTQIA+ community. He delivers so many amazing fashion looks on the red carpet, and is truly such an icon. Talking in 2021, Porter spoke about his journey of identity:

> It has been an evolution over the 52 years of my life. And it will continue to evolve. It's something that hopefully deepens with age and deepens with the right kind of work, healing work and presence. I'm still on the road to full acceptance, but I'm doing pretty good.[6]

Billy Porter brings so much joy and excellence to the world, and we are lucky to have him. He is truly a huge role model for all of us!

Key Takeaways from this Chapter

- ♥ Working out who you are can take a long time – this is okay.
- ♥ Questioning is a helpful word if you haven't fully worked out your gender identity yet.
- ♥ Repeat after me: 'I am perfect'.
- ♥ We're not fixed; we're always evolving.
- ♥ There is no pressure to come to any decisions about your gender.
- ♥ Sometimes common phrases like 'Good things take time' can be very helpful.

- ♥ When it comes to figuring yourself out, it is all about letting it take its time.
- ♥ Be more like the tortoise and less like the hare!
- ♥ There is help out there – you don't need to figure all these things out alone!

Complete the Sentences

There are some key messages in this chapter. It is very helpful to try and remember some of them when you feel like questioning yourself. To help you remember, have a go at completing the sentences below by joining them – the first one has already been done for you...

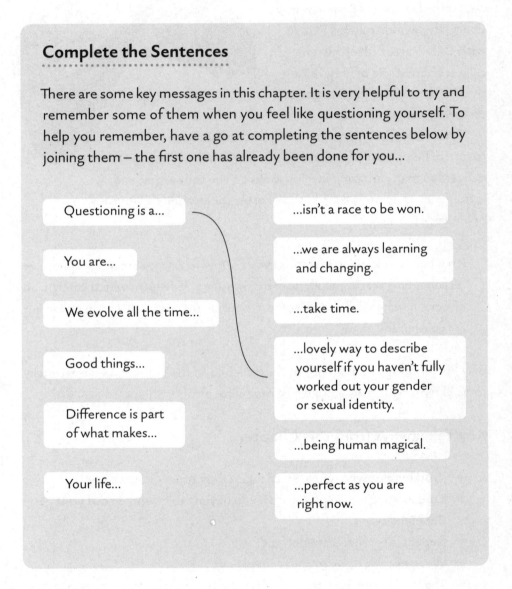

Questioning is a...	...isn't a race to be won.
You are...	...we are always learning and changing.
We evolve all the time...	...take time.
Good things...	...lovely way to describe yourself if you haven't fully worked out your gender or sexual identity.
Difference is part of what makes...	...being human magical.
Your life...	...perfect as you are right now.

Chapter 6

Feeling Lonely? Read This!

n the previous chapter we explored the idea of change on a personal level. We have also spent time thinking about how you might feel, questions you may have, and how that can begin to feel very pressured. After beginning to unlock some of these feelings, you may now feel like you have a huge secret or a burden that weighs you down.

This feeling can make you feel isolated, alone and lonely. I have been there, and it was scary, but things don't need to be like this for you. This chapter is here to make you see that your future is bright and full of joy.

In this chapter we will:

- Explore why sometimes being part of the LGBTQIA+ community can be isolating.
- Get to grips with loneliness.
- Look at the reasons why you don't need to change.
- Oh, and, of course, we can't forget about who to talk to!

I don't want you to feel alone any longer, so let's get straight on with this chapter.

Being Part of the LGBTQIA+ Community Can Be Isolating

We begin with the uncomfortable thing we might not always want to talk about AKA the elephant in the room. Being part of the LGBTQIA+ community can be isolating. This is a fact, and I don't want to dismiss it. It would be lovely to ignore this and start the chapter on a lighter note, but sadly, life doesn't work like this.

In a traditional sense, community is used to refer to a localized group of people, like a village. This is why belonging to a community can feel like we have people all around us. This might not always be the case when we talk about the LGBTQIA+ community. We are not all together in a village or town. Which means, in our life, there may be times when we are the only community member we see or know. Add to this the fact that you might not have anyone around you to help you with your questions, and it is easy to see how you can feel so alone.

I wish I could take this away and create an easier route through this part of your journey. I don't have a magic wand, but I hope I can show you that you're not alone in this process. As we unpack the challenges that being part of the LGBTQIA+ community can throw at you, you will be able to find the positives that exist here.

It Isn't Always Easy

I don't know where you are in your journey. You may be dipping your toe into the LGBTQIA+ sea, with questions and nervous anticipation. Or you may have dived in head first, knowing exactly what you want and who you want to be. It doesn't matter where you are, there will be days that are easier than others.

As far as we have come as a community, there are still quite a few sticking points that can be a little bit rubbish. Whether these are problems with your peers, family or the place where you live, it can all get on top of you. There may be times where you feel out of touch with the world around you. I wish I didn't have to type these words, but this is one of the harder parts of growing up in the LGBTQIA+ community.

Loneliness and You

The struggles we have begun to talk about can affect you in many different ways. Struggling to come to terms with your identity can make you feel lonely.

Loneliness is often described as being alone – no surprises there. The media likes us to think about loneliness in relation to others. Around winter festivities they play us adverts of older people who may be alone over the holidays. This idea of loneliness only applying to those who are on their own is not helpful.

Being lonely is actually being surround by other people, and still feeling alone. When there are few people around you who understand and support you, it is easy to feel like you are alone. In an ideal world we wouldn't have to talk about this. We don't live in an ideal world, sadly, so I want to make sure you have the right information to help you succeed as an LGBTQIA+ individual.

Perhaps You're Not Lonely — You're Just You!

It is worth considering that the sense of loneliness you may feel might not be you. To be clear, I am not suggesting that you're feeling another person's emotions. Instead, perhaps, the magical nature of being you has yet to reach the others around you!

Being yourself, sadly, is not recognized universally as a good thing. Grown-ups really like to force how they feel, or how they were brought up, on other people. This means your greatness, the things that make you wonderful, can cause others to feel negative emotions. They may not like being outshined, and instead of being supportive, they make you feel rubbish.

Being yourself can feel lonely, but it's not you — it's other people and situations making you feel like that. So don't think you are a problem, because, as we explored earlier, you are perfect just as you are.

Being 'Different' Is No Bad Thing

There are words in the English language that have many meanings. One of the main ways 'different' is used is to indicate how far away from the main group in society you are. This is an isolating term, suggesting that you don't fit in. 'Different' can be seen as a bad thing – which, if you ask me, is really stupid.

'Different' is often used with the word 'normal'. I don't know how to describe normal to you – because normal doesn't really exist! When it comes to people, there are so many questions! What is normal? What is different? The very nature of people is that we are unique. Using different in a negative way is so stupid – because humans are all different, and that is what makes life exciting.

Difference is celebrated in the LGBTQIA+ community, and in these pages. I hope that you can see the beauty in difference and celebrate that in yourself.

Who To Talk To

I know I keep mentioning common phrases, but there are some that I always come back to. I really like the next one, as it is actually helpful: *'A problem shared is a problem halved'*. Finding someone to talk to about how you are feeling is a healthy way of making that subject feel a little less scary.

We have discussed that you're not alone in feeling how you feel. Which means, there may be people around you who have similar experiences. Reaching out to people at home can feel scary, so, maybe you want to speak to someone without risking your relationship?

Finding a trusted adult at school can be a great way to get some advice. They will listen to you and the questions you may have. They may also connect you with other students in your school who may be able to support you. They will also be able to point you in the right direction of knowledge. Whether this is books or websites, this trusted adult will help you find other pieces of information to help.

Maybe you have a friend whose parents are part of the LGBTQIA+ community. Speaking to someone like this will be less formal than at school. Knowing someone like this is very lucky – because they will have lived experience and will have been in similar situations to you. This can be a very helpful way of developing the relationship you have with the LGBTQIA+ community and yourself.

There are also so many wonderful organizations that have options for you. There are helplines you can call, numbers you can text and websites you can explore. You don't have to use your name, and some websites have options for you to close pages very quickly if others are around and you aren't ready to talk about this with your family yet. There is a very helpful list of lots of organizations that can help you in Chapter 13, 'Useful Resources'.

People at Home Don't Always Understand

In the last section you may have noticed that I didn't mention the people at home for you as someone to talk to. This was intentional. I say this with care and compassion – but sometimes grown-ups don't always understand children. This is for many reasons, like growing up in an environment with little diversity (diversity means lots of different people), or perhaps they had guardians with very strong views. Whatever the reason, some adults can struggle with children who have less traditional approaches to gender and sexuality.

Of course, I have never met your family – if I have, do say 'hello' from me! So I don't know how open and accepting they are. If you know that they are supportive of the LGBTQIA+ community, then they will be a wonderful guiding hand to help you. If, on the other hand, you have heard them say things that are less than nice about the LGBTQIA+ community, you might want to avoid these conversations for now.

When I was younger, I don't remember feeling that I could speak my mind to my parents. It wasn't until I was much older that I felt able to talk to them about my gender identity. I am not suggesting that you will have a frosty reception; instead, I am showing you the reason it may happen. Don't forget to look at the resources at the end of this book (Chapter 13) and refer to the previous section to find other people to talk to until you are ready to think about talking with your family.

It Will Work Out

Being a grown-up feels like an amazing thing when you're young. I remember being desperate to grow up, to be older, wiser and free. The funny thing is, when you grow up, you might miss being young! Life can be a little more complicated as we take on more responsibility, with less time for fun. However, one thing that is worth looking forward to is that most things will work out.

The reason most things do begin to work out? Time! Time is similar to gender. It exists because people have always said it has – so, like gender, time is a social construct. Time is personal to all of us, and it shapes us. Over time, things change, grow, fade, develop or disappear. The way you and others feel right now about you will change over time.

Time has a funny way of healing wounds. Time is vital when it comes to getting used to new ideas or feelings. Time offers us perspective, the ability to see things in a different light. It might not be clear right now how you are moving forward with your life. But time will be a friend to you, as it helps you see things in new and exciting ways. So give things time. It will work out.

Role Model: Claude Cahun (they/she)

Born in 1894, Claude Cahun is one of the most historical role models I will share with you. Claude was an artist, photographer and sculptor. Their work was political and explored gender though self-portraiture and use of different characters in their work.

Their work aimed to bend the very rigid rules of gender that existed at the time. In their book, *Disavowals*, Claude explored the idea of the different personalities and gender roles we all possess.

They said: 'Under this mask, another mask. I will never be finished removing all these faces.'[7] It is clear that through their art, Claude was able to grasp the complex relationship humans have with gender – and how we are all able to define this for ourselves.

They have gone on to inspire musicians such as David Bowie, who also has a legacy of exploring gender through art and music. Claude Cahun is an historical LGBTQIA+ figure who inspires and reminds us we stand on the shoulders of giants.

Key Takeaways from this Chapter

- ♥ Being part of the LGBTQIA+ community can be isolating – but it is not just you – you are never alone!
- ♥ You're not alone; you just might not have the right people around you yet!
- ♥ If others are being tricky, remember that the magical nature of being you has yet to reach them.
- ♥ Being 'different' is no bad thing.
- ♥ There is no such thing as 'normal'.
- ♥ A problem shared is a problem halved!
- ♥ Finding someone you can trust and talk to will really help you.
- ♥ Some family members can struggle with less traditional approaches to gender and sexuality – this is okay.
- ♥ Time will be a friend to you, as it helps you see things in new and exciting ways. So give things time. It will work out.

Reflect on Your Thoughts

Using the hand mirror below, you can begin to reflect on your feelings after reading this chapter. How do you feel? What feels different? Is there something that you feel better about?

Chapter 7

What's in Your Wardrobe?

Clothing has been part of how people judge us for a very long time. Society and the way it sets out the rules has controlled what people are supposed to wear for years. Really what we wear has very little impact on our day-to-day, but we have learned to consider it a much bigger deal.

Clothing is a great tool of expression – using what you wear to say something about yourself. So when it comes to gender and the way we look, clothing can be a big help.

In this chapter we will:

- Explore that clothes have no gender.
- Get to grips with desire and the way you want to dress.
- Look at how we can be comfortable trying new things.
- Oh, and, of course, we can't forget about clothes making us happy!

Clothes Have No Gender

I don't know if you have ever noticed this, but clothes have no gender. It very rarely says a gender in the back or on the label. So when you take away the idea that clothes have gender, all you are left with is fabric, zips, buttons and thread. Which makes me think – why do clothes and what we wear cause such issues?

Clothing only has 'meaning' because of society and the rule makers. We only think a dress is for girls because someone else has told us. In reality, anyone can wear a dress, because it is just a dress, and nothing else. The same with suits, skirts, trousers, heels, corsets, ties, lederhosen, and any other clothes you can think of.

It might be the first time you have heard this, but wear what you want.

The only question you ever have to ask yourself is, 'Do I like this?' That is all that matters. As with so many of the topics we will talk about in this book, the issue is other people's feelings and not you at all. There are no rules when it comes to clothes – it is all up to you!

Clothes Can Be a Tool for Expression

While clothes may have no gender, they can have a voice. I don't mean that your jumper is going to start chatting to you about the weather! Instead, the way we choose to dress can say something about our personality.

It is very exciting to explore your personality, gender and place in the world through the clothes you choose to wear – allowing the very fabric you wear to represent you, show what you love, your passions, and, of course, explore your gender identity a little bit too.

When I was growing up it was very difficult to step outside of how others expected you to dress. It is a little easier today, but it can still be difficult. However, by using clothes to be part of your self-expression, you begin to create a chain reaction – like dominoes knocking each other over. Or a stone making ripples in a pond. This will show your friends and people around you that dressing for yourself is fun, and also, that it is exciting to ignore the 'rules'.

Your clothes can act as an advertisement for acceptance. You could kickstart a movement of dressing for you and only you. How exciting would that be?

What Is Normal Anyway?

We talked about the idea of 'normal' in the last chapter. In reality there can be no such thing as normal, because we are all different. Yet in society, clothing can be a way to group people. The way we look can be used to put us into boxes by people with less experience of difference.

As we discussed, clothing has no gender – it is just fabric. Yet a lot of other people really cling on to outdated ideas of what certain people should wear. What is silly is that over centuries, clothing trends have changed so much. What was once considered acceptable for people changes all the time.

In the late 15th century a men's fashion craze dictated that they wear long pointy shoes known as poulaines. The wealthiest had the longest – so long they had to tie the end of the shoes to their legs with chains. Up until the Victorian period all children wore dresses, pleated skirts and tunics, regardless of gender – until the age of three or four. In the 16th century men were expected to wear hose (kind of like tights) with short trousers to be fashionable – in an era where women couldn't show any leg at all.

History shows us that trends come and go – so what we wear today will always change. Choosing to wear what you like instead of following trends is good for you – it will make you happy – although I don't think shoes tied to your legs are very practical!

Desire Is Good

Desire is defined as 'a strong wish to have or do something'. Desire is important to people, as it helps us to focus on the things we want. The things we want can become the things that motivate us. This helps us set goals and have a purpose in our lives.

Desire is considered good by many. This has limits, and is usually only acceptable when talking about career, money or houses. Desire, when it comes to the way we dress, is seen as less important. This means that some people think desiring to dress a certain way is silly or pointless. The idea that desiring to look a certain way is wasted energy is very silly in my opinion. Don't listen to those people, because they're wrong.

I love desire as an emotion. Desire is brilliant, because it helps us find the things we truly love. Desire is like a magnet – it is attracted to the things we like. Unlike magnets, though, when it comes to clothes, there is no negative attraction, only positive attraction.

So don't be afraid of desire. Instead, allow desire to guide you towards the way you want to dress!

Ideal World vs. Real World

Desire is one thing; having access is another. I know clothes cost money, and perhaps that is controlled by the grown-ups in your life. But you may be able to find ways around that.

Look at the things you already own with fresh eyes. How can you change the way they feel? Can you layer them in a new way? Can you try wearing them with different things from your wardrobe? If you have permission, you could swap clothes with friends. Look around charity shops, which have options for a few pounds – maybe you'll find your new favourite garment!

Schools are also looking at the way uniforms can reflect new approaches to gender. So you could ask your school what options are open to you and your friends – trousers instead of skirts? Jumpers instead of blazers?

If you feel comfortable, speak to the grown-ups in your life, and explain how some small changes would make you feel. Together you might make it work for you!

Get Comfortable

No matter how much we want to try new things, it isn't always straightforward. When we first pull on that exciting garment, it might not feel as comfortable as we had first imagined. I don't mean comfortable in the way it feels physically, but how it makes you feel emotionally. The first time we try new things it can be a little bit scary.

One of the main reasons for this is fear. Not fear of the clothing item – unless you are scared of jumpers, in which case, don't wear them! I mean fear of judgement from other people. The way new things make us feel is always more to do with the people around us rather than how we feel.

It is far easier to wear new things when no one else is around, but it is harder in a room full of family. We have already explored how difficult other people can be. In truth, there is no remedy for this – I can't make everyone else disappear! However, it is important to remember in moments like this: *it's not you, it's them!*

You aren't scared; the other people are! They might judge you because of their own fear of change or something being a little different. That is on them, though, and shouldn't be something you need to worry about. It can be hard at first, but over time it gets so much easier.

Things to Try

When we want to explore ourselves through clothes, it can be difficult to know where to start. So here are a few things to help you try new things in comfort and safety!

- Do you feel comfy?
  Comfort really is very important – and this time I mean physical comfort. If you put clothes on and you don't like the way they feel, they are never going to work for you. Always check for comfort first.

- Try it at home.
  When something feels new and scary, going out into the world on day one is never a good idea. When I was younger my mum would always make me break in my school shoes in the last week of the summer holidays. By the time I wore them to school they'd be comfy. Try new things at home first, so when you get to wear them out you will feel super-comfy!

- Don't rush.
  There is no easy way to say this, but exploring yourself through clothes can take a long time. There is no need to rush, as we talked about before – good things take time. Allow yourself to develop over time – you will thank yourself later.

- Risk is good.
  Risks are always suggested to be bad. I don't think risks are bad – in fact, risks are the way we find new things to love. Maybe it is riskier to not take risks! So take risks – it will be fun!

- Take pictures.
  One way to chart your process and growth is through photographs. Taking pictures of different outfits is a great way to help you see what works and what doesn't – as well as exploring your journey with clothes!

Being Happy Isn't Selfish

Happiness is something we all understand. However, some people forget that happiness doesn't always equal the same thing for all of us. My happiness is not the same as yours. This is good – and another important part of being human. Some people forget that happiness is unique. When they see someone doing things to make them happy that is different from their idea of happiness, they begin to throw words like 'selfish' around.

Selfishness is often seen as a bad thing. It isn't brilliant when it ignores other people's needs. However, being a little bit selfish – which means looking out for your own happiness – is a good thing. Allowing yourself to be happy, through the way you dress, is a good thing and shouldn't be ignored.

Dressing how you want isn't a bad thing. Some people may suggest it is self-obsessed – which means only thinking about yourself – but it isn't this at all. It isn't really that selfish either. Dressing how you want is great, because it allows more joy to exist in your life. This is a good thing when we consider just how hard it can be when you are part of the LGBTQIA+ community.

So, whether others love it or not doesn't matter. All that matters is your happiness – and I hope you remember that!

Wonderful Wardrobe Moments

Sometimes all it takes is one piece of clothing to help the puzzle pieces come together. I want to share some words of wisdom from community members on the clothes that made sense for their gender identity...

My First Dress.

Cost: £2.50

Feeling: Epic awesomeness!

As I stood in front of the mirror I felt like I could finally see the other version of me I had been missing. The fluidity in my gender presentation was confirmed. The security in my non-binary nature was reached. I wish I had not waited so long. Clothes do not determine who you are or who you will be. They are there as a tool to help you express yourself and make you feel happy. *Georgie Tyrone, they/he*

When I was 11 years old and dressing up in my dad's clothes (a pair of baggy jeans and a blue check shirt) for a school play. I felt what I can only describe as an unexpected, full-body jolt as I looked in the mirror before leaving the dressing room. At the time I had no idea why, and I think I put it down to seeing myself in a 'strange' outfit, or maybe nerves about being on stage. Now I look back on it as the first time I saw my real self. *Max Slack, he/they*

The first item of clothing that affirmed my gender was a pair of grungy ankle boots. I think they were black and they were very different from the Mary Jane shoes and pink dresses my mother insisted on dressing me in for church. I remember being obsessed with those boots because they looked like the ones that the coolest girl in school wore. There was also something about these boots that was different. I had chosen them for myself and they were cool, rough and ready. They weren't like what the boys wore. Not like what the girls wore either. Something about that felt juuuuuuust right! *Yassine Senghor, she/her*

It was a leather jacket, which sounds very uneventful, I'm sure, but this jacket was unlike any other I had seen before. This was the era of the Pussycat Dolls, Lady Gaga and Rihanna, and I had found a jacket to rival them all! One shoulder was completely bedazzled, chains and spikes and rhinestones, it was absolutely perfect and I swished it down the street as I walked and felt amazing. *Dani St James, she/her*

I used to wear shirts, ties and suit jackets when I was as young as five in the land of make-believe where it was considered acceptable because when I went out into the world I was put in my little summer dress for school. I remember when I wore my shirts and ties, I felt so much more comfortable and happier. It's only in these last few years that I have finally returned to wearing the clothes I wore back then having been so distanced from myself for such a long time. Because gender stereotypes are so often associated to clothing or aesthetic that I say that my clothes affirm my identity but not so much my gender. Passing as male but identifying as non-binary, I refer to just my expression without referring to my gender. So, I don't know if the clothes I wear necessarily reflect my gender, they're just the clothes that feel comfortable on my body. *Jude Guaitamacchi, they/them*

Role Model: Alok Vaid-Menon (they/them)

Alok Vaid-Menon is a writer, performer and public speaker. Their work has received international success as they explore themes such as belonging, being human and trauma – the difficult things that have happened to us. Growing up in rural Texas, Alok faced the struggles many of us do in small communities. They now aim to teach compassion and understanding to a world that lacks both:

I'm a love poet trying to do my part in ending the international crisis of loneliness. I love trans and nonbinary people more than they [gender critical people – find out more in Chapter 8] could ever hate us. I love humanity in all of its contradictions. And most importantly – I love and need you (all of you).[8]

They are an inspiring icon within the community. They use love and compassion in a way that unites us as a community, highlighting our strength together rather than separate. Alok is doing so much for the community – we are forever in their debt!

Key Takeaways from this Chapter

- ♥ Clothing has no gender!
- ♥ Your clothes can act as an advert for acceptance.
- ♥ Pointy shoes that have to be tied to your legs are not practical!
- ♥ Desire is brilliant, because it helps us find the things we truly love.
- ♥ Others may judge you because of their own fear of change or something being a little different.
- ♥ Remember that comfort is key!
- ♥ Don't be scared of risks.
- ♥ Being a little bit selfish is a good thing.
- ♥ At the end of the day, all that matters is your happiness.

Fashion Help!

Now you have become more comfortable dressing how you want, maybe you will be able to help others too? Janice, Sasha and Fred are looking to try some new things – can you help them find them? Connect the person to the correct item by adding a line!

Janice (she/her)
Wants some fancy party shoes to feel fun and smart

Sasha (they/she)
Wants to explore more fitted structured garments

Fred (they/them)
Wants practical clothes for every day that allows them to move freely

Chapter 8

A Town Called Barriers

Okay, we're at a big chapter. Not big, lengthwise. More that we need to talk about a big subject. So far we have explored gender identities, questions you may have, how you may feel, loneliness and dressing for joy.

These chapters have all been very personal. In a way, they have all been about you — and things in your control. Where we are heading next is very much out of your control. In fact, it is out of control full stop. We are going to take a train ride to the town of Barriers — where things for LGBTQIA+ people are tricky — really tricky.

It isn't a place any of us want to visit, but sadly it is a place we have to be aware of. So buckle up as we take a whistle-stop tour of the sights in the town of Barriers!

In this chapter we will:

- Explore the murky world of gender critics.
- Get to grips with why some people are scared of the LGBTQIA+ community.
- Look at transphobia.
- Oh, and, of course, we can't forget about how much better things are!

Gender Critics

Our first stop on the tour of Barriers is to a place that has become more popular recently. We are talking about gender critics. Gender critics are people who have very strong negative opinions of gender identities outside of cisgender men and women. This is usually expressed in a way that suggests that trans and non-binary people are a threat to cisgender women.

These people are very vocal online. They usually operate on social media platforms like Twitter, Facebook and Instagram. Sometimes they create conversations usually based on misinformation or even lies. Other times they comment on content created by trans and non-binary people.

It is worth mentioning that everyone is entitled to an opinion. This is part of being human. However, it doesn't give anyone the right to be horrible to another person based on their gender identity or expression. There is no way we can even begin to deal with some of the unpleasant behaviour created by gender critics. But it can be helpful to understand where this negativity comes from.

Fight or Flight

The response that LGBTQIA+ people and more specifically the trans community face from gender critics can be traced back through thousands of years of life on Earth. We talked about our ancestor *Homo erectus* in Chapter 5. Back then, life on Earth was much more basic. Without the convenience of the app store, online shopping or supermarkets, events like lunch could be life or death!

This is why humans have a hormonal response – chemicals triggered by our brains that cause our behaviour to change – to help us stay safe. One of these responses is known as the 'fight or flight'. This helped humans of the past determine if animals, plants, other people and situations were dangerous or not.

The fact that we are on Earth today is thanks to our ancestors' fight or flight response. Knowing whether to run away from a woolly mammoth or not to eat certain berries is all down to this hormonal response. So what does fight or flight have to do with gender critics? Well, the key factor that triggers this response is difference.

Difference is something that we have talked about. When some people grow up only seeing people like them, meeting a trans community member for the first time can trigger a person's fight or flight response because a trans person is a new experience. Now most people will get over their initial response, and realize that gender-diverse people are just like them.

Gender critics use their fear response to become hateful and unpleasant to gender-diverse people, because they refuse to learn and accept difference. This is where the gender critics get all their energy from – a primeval hormonal response. Not only is this outdated; it is also very narrow-minded. Which is why the next stop on our tour of Barriers is so important when it comes to reducing the amount of gender critics in existence.

Visibility

If a tree falls in a forest and no one is around to hear it, does it make a sound? This is a philosophical question – which means it is thought-provoking and allows us to question the things we experience in life. In relation to the LGBTQIA+ community, you could ask: can you be trans and non-binary if you have never seen somebody like that?

In reality, of course you can be LGBTQIA+ without any outside influence. However, it is much harder to work out how to be a member of the community when you can't see any representation in the world around you. We have come a long way in the 21st century, and there is more visibility for gay men but perhaps less for the rest of the community.

Without visibility it is very hard for us to feel like we have a place to belong. Less visibility creates more opportunities for gender critics to exist. The lack of visibility that the community has is one

of the biggest barriers any of us face. Until significant changes are made, this vicious cycle of lack of visibility creating gender critics will continue to happen.

Inclusion

Next on our tour of Barriers is inclusion. Inclusion, on the face of it, is a good thing. Inclusion is all about including people in conversations, the media we consume and wider things people interact with. Just like visibility, the community has done a lot to make many more instances of inclusion happen. However, it doesn't really cut the mustard at the moment.

Advertising can be a very big way inclusion can create visibility. However, brands and companies are always getting this wrong. They either do it once and never do it again, or they pick very specific identities to represent and create a very narrow story – which could look like including disabled people in an advert, but only letting them talk about being disabled, and not that they are fluent in six languages and are a chess champion!

Inclusion is the best friend of visibility – but is so very badly misunderstood. Without proper knowledge of inclusion, and what this should look like, brands, businesses and media can really misrepresent the LGBTQIA+ community. This means that what little representation we get as a community could be full of incorrect information that causes non-community members to expect us to act a certain way. Bad inclusion can be a huge barrier for us.

Bullying

I really didn't like school. I never really fitted in, and, in fact, struggled every day. The main reason for this was how I was treated by my peers. Very sadly, when people spot differences, they like to highlight them in a negative way. This is called bullying. You may have experienced this in your life.

Bullying on its own is hard, but when it is done in a large group, like at school, it can group people, creating divides. This divide tends to create a group of popular people, and some who are less popular. As a member of the LGBTQIA+ community there is a chance you will face some bullying from those outside of the community. It is one of the harder parts of growing up.

Some describe this bullying as a rite of passage – which means when an individual undergoes an event that helps them develop into the person they are now. This is not right, and bullying should never be tolerated at any level, at any age. Bullying is nothing small, or anything to be ignored. If you are struggling with bullying, make sure you speak to a trusted adult or use the resources at the end of this book (see Chapter 13) to get help from various organizations. You are never alone, and you shouldn't suffer in silence.

Transphobia

Next on our tour of Barriers is transphobia. It is somewhere I wish we didn't have to visit, but sadly it is part of being in the LGBTQIA+ community in the UK today. Transphobia is hatred directed towards trans people. It also exists to limit the access trans people have to basic things such as work and healthcare.

There is no nice way to phrase it, because transphobia sits in a group of behaviours that are really terrible. It exists alongside homophobia (hatred and different treatment of gay men and lesbians), biphobia (hatred and different treatment of bisexual people) and racism (hatred and different treatment of people due to where they come from, cultural background, nationality or colour of their skin).

Transphobia is nothing new, but it has become more talked about recently. As visibility has grown for trans people, so has the abuse they receive. People who are transphobic are known colloquially as transphobes. The gender critics we explored earlier are the number one transphobes.

Transphobic behaviour centres on the idea that trans people cannot exist. There are a few reasons they use. First, religion is used, suggesting that 'God doesn't make mistakes' – and so no one can be born in the wrong body. Another reason is science – 'our body parts are the only way gender can be expressed' – so no one can change their gender. Some transphobes like to say that non-binary people are just confused girls and boys.

All of these reasons and views are just opinions. They are not facts. There is no proof for any transphobic opinions. Quite often transphobic people and literature quote information that is false, or not fully researched. Transphobia in general loves to use fake news to push its agenda.

This doesn't take the sting away from the way transphobia can affect you, but it can help you to understand it. We don't know why people use hatred against certain groups – but it is a big part of our society. Understanding that it exists, and how much of it is personal opinion and untruths, can help you ignore some of it.

If you are reading this, and you don't identify within the trans community, it is never acceptable to be transphobic. If you see it happening, you should try and stop it. It can be hard, but it is much harder for trans people to deal with alone. We will talk more about this later on, when we discuss allyship in a couple of chapters' time.

The Problem with the Media

We are surrounded by media – TV, news, social media and the internet. This media plays a role in all our lives, shaping and affecting them. Twenty years ago, the main characters were the newspapers; now it is all online, with written articles becoming the way the world talks about key issues. One such 'issue' is, of course, trans people, and the wider LGBTQIA+ community. These articles, often very opinion-based, become part of the conversation about our community in wider society, and are believed as if fully truthful and factual.

It means that lots and lots of articles are written by cisgender people, who also happen to have views that are transphobic, biphobic and sometimes homophobic. These articles are then treated as if they are full of facts and contain nothing but the truth. It is scary how quickly these opinions become rules trans people must follow.

It is very hard to stop this happening, because we are all allowed freedom of speech – the ability to speak our mind. However, when you come across media that is negative about the community, ask yourself a few questions to ensure you're reading the truth:

- Who wrote this article? If this person is not trans, how experienced are they to talk about this?
- Has the author spoken to trans people? If there is no community involved, it is probably not true!
- Where was the article published? Does the website normally support the community? If not, then this is unlikely to be a positive thing to read.

It can be hard to see, but knowing what is good and bad media can help you in not being exposed to harmful content online.

It's Not a Perfect World

There are laws and legislation that are in operation to help LGBTQIA+ people. One of these is the Equalities Act. This was created in 2010, to update lots of other individual laws and acts. The Equalities Act aims to protect nine characteristics: age, disability, gender reassignment, marriage and civil partnership, pregnancy and maternity, race, religion or belief, sex, and sexual orientation.

On paper this is a good thing, as it helps protect LGBTQIA+ people when it comes to sex, gender and sexual orientation. However, this same law can be used as a defence for transphobic opinions and ideas expressed by individuals.

So there are pros and cons to the Equalities Act – it can be helpful, but it can also be a barrier. It is always worth knowing how you can be protected, and how certain individuals can twist that, too.

Things Aren't Perfect, But They Are Much Better

I have just talked about a piece of law that can be used for and against the LGBTQIA+ community. Things aren't perfect, but they are better than they used to be. When I was at school, a piece of legislation called Section 28 was in operation. This legislation prevented schools and local authorities from talking about, educating and promoting LGBTQIA+ information.

This came into effect in 1988 when the then prime minister, Margaret Thatcher, used Section 28 to promote 'traditional values' and move away from what the government called 'pretended family relationships' that the LGBTQIA+ community represented to them. It was very popular with voters, and stayed in effect until 2000 in Scotland, and 2003 in Wales and England.

Growing up under Section 28, and the lasting effects that existed for years after, created generations of LGBTQIA+ people who knew very little about the community and the people they were. Now LGBTQIA+ rights and community members are celebrated in small ways in schools and local authorities. It isn't perfect, but it is much better than when Section 28 was law.

So, although the way things are now isn't perfect, they are a lot better than they used to be. Big or small, we should always be grateful for progress.

Role Model: Paris Lees (she/her)

Raised in Nottinghamshire, writer, presenter and columnist Paris Lees is a trailblazer for the trans community. She was the first openly trans presenter on BBC Radio One and Channel 4, and has appeared in British *Vogue*.

With a difficult childhood leading to some bad choices in her teens, Paris turned her life around on her own terms, channelling the power of doing it her way. Paris is a prime example of a self-made person.

Paris is a force for good in this world, and has a stance that trans people are more than just statistics or newsworthy soundbites: 'I'm more than just a trans person, and I refuse to regurgitate a misery narrative for cis people's consumption.'[9]

She has gone on to win awards, write books, and even star in adverts on TV. Paris is a fresh, exciting, iconic member of our community, and is rightly a role model.

Key Takeaways from this Chapter

- ♥ No one has the right to be horrible to another person based on their gender identity or expression.
- ♥ Some responses to LGBTQIA+ people are caused by prehistoric behaviour.
- ♥ The lack of visibility that the community has is one of the biggest barriers any of us face.
- ♥ Paired with visibility, inclusion can be a huge help for the community — but more needs to be done.

- ♥ Bullying is never okay. You are never alone, and you shouldn't suffer in silence.
- ♥ Transphobia loves fake news – so don't believe any of it.
- ♥ There is no excuse for transphobia – allies can always do something about it!
- ♥ Knowing what is good and bad media can help you to not be exposed to negative energy online.
- ♥ Things may not be as good as they could be right now. Generally they are better than they used to be. This can give us all hope.

Barriers Quiz

This chapter was heavy going – we have covered some very big subjects together. There are plenty of very powerful grown-ups who don't know half the things that you have just read – so I wouldn't blame you if you feel a bit overwhelmed!

To help some of the key facts sink in a little better, I have created a mini quiz to see how much you can remember, and to show you what you might need to spend a little more time looking at again. Good luck!

1. What reaction in our bodies makes new things seem scary?
   a. Hunger
   b. Fight or flight
   c. Exercise

2. What is missing that makes it very hard for us to feel like we have a place to belong?
   a. Visibility
   b. Lunch
   c. Adverts

3. Transphobia isn't...?
   a. Real
   b. Alive
   c. Fact

4. Bullying is not a...?
    a. Rite of passage
    b. Holiday
    c. Bouncy castle

5. Which legislation was scrapped in 2003 in Wales and England?
    a. The Equalities Act
    b. Section 28
    c. The Hokey Cokey

Chapter 9

When Was the Last Time You Were Happy?

Happiness is really important. If you take happiness away from life, all life really is, is chores and sleeping. Without happiness life is like a black and white film. Happiness is that missing element. Happiness brings all the colour into our life. So it is my responsibility to make sure I help you find as much happiness as I can.

As you have read my words, you will have picked up on some of the negative elements we have discussed. These are some of the things that can alter your happiness levels. I can't make those go away, sadly. I can, however, give you some tips to increase your happiness levels, even in the face of the barriers we all experience.

In this chapter we will:

- Explore our mental health, and what that means.
- Get to grips with why technology isn't the most important thing.
- Look at distractions.
- Oh, and, of course, we can't forget about the importance of sleep!

Happiness Is Not a Fixed State

First things first. We need to unpack happiness as an emotion. When we think of happiness, we often confuse it with things that are permanent. Permanent things are always there, like Mondays, or our need to eat and drink. Happiness isn't permanent, because people cannot be happy all the time.

Special things aren't special if we have them all the time. That is why things like holidays and birthday cakes are so lovely – because they are something we don't have all the time. It would be nice to be happy all the time, but if we were, happiness wouldn't be special any more.

Knowing that we don't need to be happy all the time is important. It helps us all learn that life is full of ups and downs. These ups and downs are part of the things we love, and love less, in life. Someone being born is a happy event, the death of a loved one is a sad event – these are the ups and downs of life.

We have discussed barriers – the things in the lives of LGBTQIA+ people that are not nice – these are the downs we face. Good things make us happy, just like birthday cake. There is more good than bad in our lives, which means there is much more room for happiness. You just need to know where to look for it. Keep reading to find out!

Mental Health and You

Mental health is being talked about a lot. It isn't new, but it is getting more attention than it used to. Mental health is the way we think about ourselves and the world around us. When our mental health changes, either because of emotion or the way a person thinks, it can affect how we feel.

It doesn't just happen inside our heads. If we get nervous or scared, it can make our heart beat faster, or make us feel sick. When this has a negative impact on us, we call this mental ill health. Mental ill health is harder to treat than broken bones or headaches, because it can have many causes.

Here are some of the things that can affect your mental health:

- Changes, like moving house and a new school
- Bullying
- Parents who are divorcing
- Difficulties learning at school
- Winter – darker, shorter days
- Daily stress – scared of your maths teacher etc.

You might notice a change in how you feel. This might not be anything to worry about, but if you are worried, then you can do a few things to ensure you are looking after your mental health. You could talk to a friend or trusted adult. You can talk to your parents or guardian and book an appointment with your doctor. If you want things to be confidential (private), you can look at the resources at the end of this book (see Chapter 13) and get open-minded advice from several organizations.

The most important thing to know is that you're not alone, and you never need to suffer in silence.

Don't Isolate Yourself

When we feel our mood change – regardless of the reason – we can feel like other people may not understand us. The thoughts and feelings in our mind can make us sad, anxious or very worried. When we feel like this, it can be easy to shut down and ignore things and the people around us. This isn't always a very good idea.

No one can feel how you feel in the moment. However, if you explain how you feel, other people can understand. This is down to something called empathy. Empathy is the ability to understand and share the feelings of another person. Empathy is an emotional response. We don't have to have the same experiences in order to empathize (emotionally understand) another person.

Even though you may feel like isolating yourself, it is not a good idea when other people can help you. Big or small, talking about how we feel is always a good idea. Other people will be able to empathize and think of ways to help you feel better. So please don't isolate yourself.

Focus On You

One key part of mental health, and looking after yourself, is ensuring that you're okay. This sounds very simple, but with the way life currently happens, it is more complicated. We very rarely have days where we just get to focus on ourselves. There will be so many other people who are going to need your attention.

We have almost created a society where comparison is a key part of our lives. Comparison or comparing means we look at other people, their lives and the things they do or have. We then judge those things against the way we view our life, and the things we do or have. We either feel like we're better than that person, or we feel the other person is better, and we feel uncomfortable about this.

Comparison is human nature – but it is important to not give it too much focus. There is more to life than comparison and who has what. The less time you spend comparing yourself, the more time you can focus on you – and that is so vital. So remember to always focus on yourself!

The Internet Is Good, but It Isn't Everything

I don't know how often you use the internet or use apps on tablets or phones. I do know that more and more people are accessing the internet at younger ages than ever before. The internet and games can be a great way to switch off from your day. However, it is not the only thing to use.

When I use my phone for too long, I begin to feel my mood dip. I am not the only one. Scientists have found that spending too much time on screens can affect our mood, sleep, how we think, and how we feel offline, too.

There is a saying that too much of a good thing is bad. This means that if we overuse something, it becomes less effective. So if we spend too much time online, it can begin to affect us negatively. Think about this the next time too much time online makes you feel flatter than a pancake!

The Importance of Sleep

Sleep is super-important. It often gets overlooked. If you have a bad night's sleep, you will feel less than your best the next day. No one likes feeling groggy, grumpy and ghastly. Without good regular sleep we can all feel rubbish.

Sleep is so helpful. When we are asleep we are not only restoring the energy we have used. Sleep also allows our body to grow, heal and repair. So many important things happen while we are dreaming. It is no wonder we feel less than great when we don't sleep well.

Try and create some space around the time you sleep. Less screen time near bedtime is always a good thing – the light from phones and tablets can affect our sleep patterns. Routine is also good, as your body will know when you are ready to sleep.

When you grow up, somehow you never get enough time to sleep. I miss all the times as a younger person when I could sleep more! So never underestimate the importance sleep can have on your wellbeing and mental health.

Distractions Are Good

There are things you can do daily to help your mental health. One of these is distractions. They don't solve the problems fully, but give you time where you can relax and recharge your batteries. We explored that the internet is good for short bursts, but I wanted to share some other things that might distract you and put you in a better mood!

- Build a den out of blankets and cushions!
- Play in the garden
- Read or listen to a book
- Tidy up your space
- Look up some of the role models we have explored in this book at your local library
- Put some music on and have a dance
- Get creative and have a draw
- Create a new world with building bricks
- Talk to your pets
- Have a nap
- Can you help your parents or guardian out?
- Feeling green fingered? Do some gardening
- Speak to your friends
- Plan your future – list your hopes and dreams
- Save the planet and get recycling.

Feel-Good Films

I specifically left out one distraction from this list. Watching a film is one of my favourite ways to distract myself. A good film can help you unwind, relax and let your brain truly rest. There are hundreds of options out there.

I don't know what kind of films you like, but I thought I would share some films that always make me feel good!

- *Babe* – we love an underdog (well, a pig) who wins!
- *Hercules* – a classic Greek story retold through the magic of Disney.
- *Matilda* – a child who reads and succeeds – what's not to love?
- *Monsters, Inc.* – fun and silly, a great way to spend an afternoon.
- *Wall-E* – romance and recycling, a great message about our climate!
- *Aladdin* – rub the lamp and all your wishes will come true.
- *Frozen* and *Frozen 2* – let's all get lost in an exciting magical twist on a classic story.
- *Inside Out* – love seeing the dynamic of all our emotions inside our brain!
- *Mulan* – proof that gender has nothing to do with ability!
- *Bedknobs and Broomsticks* – you're never too old to learn how to be a witch!

Role Model: Travis Alabanza (they/them)

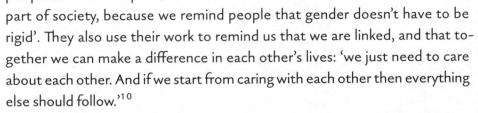

Travis Alabanza is an award-winning writer, theatre maker and performance artist. They have written several plays that centre on the experience of trans people and their safety. Their work is based on their experiences and upbringing as a queer person of colour in Bristol.

Travis's work goes beyond cisgender and trans identities, instead looking at how society treats non-conforming people as if they are failing. They also see gender, and the way we can all explore it, as fun: 'trans people are such a positive part of society, because we remind people that gender doesn't have to be rigid'. They also use their work to remind us that we are linked, and that together we can make a difference in each other's lives: 'we just need to care about each other. And if we start from caring with each other then everything else should follow.'[10]

The *Evening Standard* listed them as one of the 25 most influential under-25-year-olds, they have been included in the Dazed100, and recently made the Forbes '30 under 30' list. Travis Alabanza is a huge talent and cheerleader for the trans community — and is a true role model for all of us.

Key Takeaways from this Chapter

- ♥ We can't be happy all the time — and that's okay!
- ♥ Mental health doesn't just affect our head, but our bodies too.
- ♥ Other people can always help you — don't suffer in silence.
- ♥ We always need to make time for ourselves.
- ♥ Spend less time comparing yourself to others.
- ♥ If we spend too much time online, it can begin to affect us negatively.
- ♥ Distracting yourself can be good for your mental health.

♥ Sleep is so important – make time for it!

♥ A good film can help you unwind, relax and let your brain truly rest.

Happiness Supermarket

Happiness, as we have discussed, is not a permanent state. It can also be affected by many things. Some days we need an extra boost to help increase our mood. Knowing what these things are is helpful, and we can use them to help us cope.

I thought you could work out how to budget for this, by shopping at the Happiness Supermarket (see the illustration on the next page). I've been generous and given you £6 to spend. You can spend the full amount or less than the full amount, but not a penny more. Make sure you spend it wisely and work out how to use certain things that make you happy in your life.

Chapter 10

How to Support Your Friends

One of the most universal facts that exists is that we never know how other people feel. This is because we can only go from what they tell us. We all hold certain things back; we all have secrets. This makes it hard when we see a friend who is struggling.

You may not be the only one who is coming to terms with your gender identity. Maybe you're cisgender, reading this book specifically to understand your gender-diverse friends. Whatever your intentions, this chapter will help you find out the many ways in which you can help.

In this chapter we will:

- Explore allyship, and what that means.
- Get to grips with why it's okay to not know everything.
- Look at how we can all learn together.
- Oh, and, of course, we can't forget about the importance of apologizing when we get it wrong!

What Is an Ally?

When I was at school, I only ever heard the term 'ally' in connection to history, or wars. Allies are people who support the beliefs of another group of people. This means they act as bridges between that group and the rest of society.

Allies are very useful when it comes to gender. Allies for trans people are often cisgender people who believe that trans people are wonderful and valid. They speak up for us when we are not listened too. They make sure that our rights are protected. They can spread education, protest with us and help us be heard in spaces we may not be safe in.

In short, allies are the one thing that can help a small community like the trans community. Allies are wonderful. Allies are so vital. Allies are how we progress as a community. We need more allies. If you are reading this book and you are cisgender, then you are already well on your way to being an ally – congratulations!

Keep reading to find out what else you need to be a great ally.

You're Not a Bad Person for Not Knowing Everything!

One thing that we can experience is people who get upset that they don't know everything. This is very silly for a few reasons. First, if we knew everything, there would be no problems. Second, our heads are too small to have all the knowledge in the world inside them – you don't want your head to explode, do you?!

So, not knowing everything is part of being human – it is okay! However, when it comes to gender and the conversations we need to have to help others learn, some people get very annoyed. They don't like to be told that their worldview and understanding is wrong. They take this very personally, and assume we are telling them that they're a bad person, and switch off from all conversations to do with gender.

This means that they are not helping at all. It also means that they are not fully informed to make good decisions either! This can be a difficult mindset to shift, but it needs to be done. You are not bad for not knowing everything. You are just human.

It's Okay to Get Things Wrong!

After you have mastered not needing to know everything, we come to another issue – mistakes. Mistakes are so misunderstood. I used to be scared of mistakes, thinking them the end of the world. This was only because I didn't really know the value that mistakes add to our lives. Some people still live like this – so scared of getting things wrong that they are frozen, unable to do anything!

Mistakes are one of the biggest ways that we learn. A mistake can show you how not to act, speak, do, and so many other things. Without mistakes, we don't evolve. They are so vital to our development. To be afraid of mistakes is to be afraid of living life.

We cannot hope to never make mistakes! This is silly. Everyone makes mistakes. Politicians, grown-ups, and even the Pope! The important part of mistakes is what we do with them afterwards. As long as we learn from them, we are doing okay.

When it comes to gender, mistakes are inevitable. Whether this is the language we use, getting people's name wrong, getting muddled over pronouns – mistakes are bound to happen. However, don't be scared of them.

How to Learn from Your Mistakes

When we make mistakes it is important to ask yourself a few questions:

- How did my actions affect others?
  Did your actions upset someone else? Did you make your friend uncomfortable? Think about how your mistake may have upset someone else's day. Then think about how you would feel if you were in their shoes.

- What happened that made *this* a mistake?
  Now that you understand that you have upset or offended someone, you need to identify the action that caused this emotional response. Was it that you didn't fully understand the term you were discussing? Was it that you got muddled over pronouns? Or did you use someone's dead name (the name they were given before they transitioned)? It is important that you can identify what the mistake was so that you can ensure it doesn't happen again.

- What can I do to make sure I don't do this again?
  Now that you understand what happened, you need to try and work out how you will make it better. Do you need to do some more research on certain areas? Do you need to speak to that person later on to make sure you know their correct pronouns? Or maybe you need to say sorry to show your commitment to getting things right?

These three questions and the answers you get will help you learn from your mistakes. This will help you be a better ally and a better friend.

Say Sorry If You Get It Wrong

When we make mistakes, there is a chance that we may have hurt another person's feelings. This is also part of being human; whether we mean to or not, our actions can upset others. If you used the wrong pronouns and incorrect gender to refer to a friend, or perhaps got their name wrong, then that person may very well be upset. Just like mistakes, what we do after the event is the important thing.

Apologizing isn't easy. Not only do we have to know what we have done wrong, we also have to show we truly meant no harm. The easiest way to understand how the other person feels is to imagine how you would feel if the other person had done what you did or said to you. Now you can begin to understand their emotions, and why they might be upset.

When another person is upset, it can be easy to see an apology as an empty gesture — just something to be said to stop the situation getting worse. However, if you truly are sorry, it does have a lot of meaning. Simply saying sorry isn't always enough, as it doesn't show any changed behaviour. If you need time to understand what happened, that is okay. When you do say sorry, you will understand — and it will have true meaning.

Owning your mistakes and showing you understand what you did is very important. It shows the other person that you aren't being unkind. It also shows that you are open to learning from your mistakes. It is a very nice way to show your support for other people — and that you are an ally to them and their needs.

Try Not to Be Unkind

When we don't fully understand someone's difference, we can be confused or even scared. We talked about this in Chapter 8. Some people can use this confusion to be unkind, using the things that make people different as a way to upset them.

It is never okay to use someone's gender, sexuality, race, colour, height, body size, accent, speech, wealth or intelligence to hurt them.

Differences between people is what makes being human wonderful. If we were all the same, the world would be so boring. There would be no new ideas, and nothing would ever change. So there is no good to be gained from making another person feel bad about their differences.

Kindness isn't the lack of bad behaviour – but it is where better behaviour starts. So please try not to be unkind to others.

Try to Do Some Research

As I have mentioned, we, as people, never really know everything. School is where a lot of learning happens. But as we grow older, we need to continue to learn in order to be better people. So learning to learn all the time is a very helpful skill.

We can't know how it feels to be another person. This means we won't be able to know what it feels like to experience the world in their unique way. It is helpful to research how others may feel. A good example of this is not being part of the trans community, but reading this book to help you understand how complicated it can be.

Learning how other people experience the world is a great way to make sure you can do more to help. Read books that cover different topics that might not impact your life. Listen to other people's experiences of life, and how they might feel. Doing things like this will help you be a good ally to them.

Don't Speak for Your Friends

By now you are well on the road to being a good ally. One easy way to trip up is to assume you need to talk for a friend. Telling other people what they might need. Saying how they might feel, before they even have the chance.

You might even start being defensive towards others who you think are hurting your friend.

This is talking over someone else — and although you are trying to do the right thing, it is not actually very helpful. When we talk over people in this way, we are actually silencing them. Instead of them having the freedom to talk and express themselves, you are filling that space with your voice. This means that your friend is actually in far less control. It also makes other people treat them like they're not there — by talking to you about them — which can feel very strange.

If you care enough about someone, you will be there for them, but you don't need to speak for them. As a supportive friend you can make sure that your friend is heard, treated with respect and that they are happy. If you find yourself speaking for them, apologize and stay quiet so your friend can speak for themselves.

We all have a voice — it is important to have the space to share it!

Role Model: Charlie Craggs (she/her)

Charlie Craggs is a writer, campaigner and actress. She has worked tirelessly to try to change the world through her work, and has made such a difference in the lives of trans people. Charlie created a campaign called Nail Transphobia, which provided manicures and the chance to speak to trans people in a bid to reduce transphobia.

Charlie also successfully campaigned for the inclusion of a transgender flag in the emojis we can use on phones and computers. Charlie understands the vital need for allies:

Allies worldwide are essential in the progression of any social cause but especially in the case of trans rights, because there are so few trans people in the world. I've heard a few different numbers, but it's predicted we make up about 1 per cent of the global population, so if we really want to see a change in attitude or a change in legislation, we need allies on our side to amplify our voices and put up a united front with us.[11]

Charlie Craggs is an icon and a powerhouse, and such an important role model for all of us!

Key Takeaways from this Chapter

- ♥ Allies are people who support the beliefs of another group of people – and try to help!
- ♥ We need more allies – can you be one?
- ♥ We don't need to be upset that we don't know everything – we're human!
- ♥ It is okay to get things wrong – mistakes are good!
- ♥ We can learn from our mistakes – and become better people.
- ♥ It is important to apologize, and to learn from our actions so we don't hurt anyone else in the same way.
- ♥ It is never okay to use someone's gender, sexuality, race, colour, height, body size, accent, speech, wealth or intelligence to hurt them.
- ♥ Learning how other people experience the world is a great way to make sure you can do more to help.
- ♥ If you care enough about someone, you will be there for them, but you don't need to speak for them.

Supportive Friend Guess Who

After reading how to support your friends, it is a great time to test what you have learned. Below are four potential friends, and they all approach life differently. You need to work out which three are supportive, and which one person is not a supportive friend! Good luck!

Margaret (she/her)
Isn't scared of mistakes
Always happy to learn

Asha (she/her)
Always researches
Never speaks for others

Jamie (he/him)
Believes he's always right
Won't apologize

Teddy (they/them)
Embraces difference
Always tries to be kind

What Next? The Start of Your Gender Story

So you have made it to Chapter 11. Congratulations to you for getting here – reading is a marathon and not a sprint. We should now talk about the time you are going to spend with yourself and your friends after you read this book.

The pages of this book have held your hand as we have explored topics like gender identities, pronouns, big questions, loneliness, barriers, and so many more. These conversations don't just stop when you finish the book, and so in this chapter I want to help you create a route map to support you.

In this chapter we will:

- Explore why visibility isn't the main goal right now.
- Get to grips with tricky time.
- Talk about the importance of community elders.
- Oh, and, of course, we can't forget about the importance of celebrating *you*!

Kindness Is Key

I think we have probably looked at parts of kindness together in every chapter. However, in this chapter we will stop and explore it in a little more depth. Kindness is defined as the quality of being friendly, generous and considerate. We often think about kindness as an act that we offer other people. Yet how much time do you spend being kind to yourself?

Being kind to yourself isn't a ground-breaking act, and it won't make the world change overnight. However, when you are kind to yourself, you boost your wellbeing – or how you feel about yourself. This is very useful when it comes to important things like your self-esteem. Self-esteem is the thing that helps you feel good about yourself. Self-esteem also helps you believe in your abilities – and highlights your strengths.

Your self-esteem is there for you through the ups and downs of life. Being kinder to yourself helps your self-esteem grow, and strengthens the relationship you have with yourself. This is a good thing to have when the world around us is less than friendly to the LGBTQIA+ community. Think of being kind to yourself and strengthening your self-esteem as your own personal ally. It is a no-brainer to have this internal support – so being kind to yourself is key!

Give Yourself Time

Of course, a lot of the things that we have taken time to explore together cannot just happen overnight. Time is another piece of the conversation that should be part of your thought process. Certainly to begin with let the words I have shared with you sink in. It can take more than once for some information to actually make sense to you. As an adult, I still have to read things a few times to fully understand them.

Another element is that there may be parts of you that you are still discovering, or that feel very new to you. There will be a period of time where you feel you are still adjusting to them. This is definitely part of everybody's journey of learning who they are – so don't be afraid to feel this yourself. Getting to know new parts of your identity may feel a little strange or disorientating, but it is a natural part of being yourself.

Time is constant, and because of that, we never stay still. Whether we like it or not, time and life are always happening. This means that each day you move further on your journey, and each day will present new challenges. If you look back to six months ago, there will be things you couldn't do that you can do now, and things you were afraid of that now are nothing to worry about. Time passes and allows us to grow unconsciously – without us even noticing it.

So even if you don't put much time into thinking about where you are heading, time will make sure it is always in the direction of personal growth. Some people think time is our enemy – but I believe it to be a good friend. Time allows us all to be who we are, so let it take your hand and you will grow every day.

You Don't Need to Be Visible to Be Valid

We talked about all the ways you can identify in Chapter 3. For some of you reading this, you may already be happy with this, and be happy being you with the people around you. For some of you, you may not be ready to be so open. One part of the conversation that is often forgotten is the people who aren't able to be visible in their identity.

Whatever the reason you are not ready to be visible, it is okay to take your time with this — as we discussed earlier. However, this doesn't make your identity and how you feel any less valid — or real. It is important to remember that just because others may not see you the way you see yourself, nobody can take away how you feel.

It is not your job to create the space in the community; it is the job of the community to help make space for you. So you might not be exactly where you want to be in terms of your identity, understanding or knowledge of yourself. But it doesn't stop how you feel from being the truth. You are exactly who you feel you are — and I want you to hold on to that.

You Can't Be What You Don't See

You may not feel that you're being 100% yourself, because you're not fully visible. This is connected to a few things. One of the main things that can stop you feeling fully yourself is that you cannot be what you don't see. This means that it is harder to be something you have no examples of. It's not impossible to be you, but having no one to look up to makes it much harder.

This links back to some of the barriers we discussed in Chapter 8. A lack of visibility and inclusion — seeing and being included — means that some of us don't have any way to voice how we feel. It can also be harder to explain how you feel when there are fewer examples that can help others around you understand.

There is truth in 'you can't be what you don't see' – but it shouldn't be the thing that defines you. There are billions of people on the planet – and yet there is only one you. It can be helpful to see other people like ourselves, but there is probably no one quite like you – so you don't have to wait to see someone else to feel valid or to be yourself. You are already doing it – you are valid and you are being yourself. Time will show you who you are going to be – and you will see then what that looks like.

There Is No Rush

Life is very quick, too busy, perhaps. We all seem to be in such a rush these days. With next-day delivery, news on our devices all the time, overnight fame for reality telly stars, and fast food – there is no time to spare. This rush that we all seem to be in also applies to the journey of finding yourself. When it comes to people, rushing is never a good thing.

One thing that is different now to when I was growing up is that there is much more opportunity to be yourself right now. I didn't really figure things out for myself until I was in my twenties. However, even though I started a little later, it has still taken me years to fully work out who I am. I also know that things will change for me as I continue to discover things about myself – so I am not done on my journey.

It may not take you years and years, but it certainly won't happen over-night. Trying to rush the very important job of working out who we are will never really work properly. There is no rush, because there is no finish line – you don't have a final destination. We are all evolving every day – so why rush it, when it will happen very nicely on its own?!

The Importance of Community Elders

We stand on the shoulders of giants. Not literally – that would be weird! What this phrase means is, we owe those who have come before us. The people who fought for the rights we have, the people who used their lives to make the lives of the next generation better. These are the people who have made it easier for each next generation.

The world loves to celebrate youth, whether this is celebrity, brand-new technology or even just looking younger. Experience can come with age – the longer you have lived, the more you can know. This may not be applicable for all walks of life, but when it comes to the LGBTQIA+ community, there are countless people we can all look up to who have made it possible for us to be who we want to be right now. Some we have already discussed, and some are new to you – but all are very important people you should know:

- Marsha P. Johnson
- Phyllis Akua Opoku-Gyimah, better known as Lady Phyll
- Peter Tatchell
- Sylvia Rivera
- Munroe Bergdorf
- Alan Turing
- Bayard Rustin
- Paris Lees
- Stormé DeLarverie
- James Baldwin
- Shon Faye
- Barbara Gittings.

Explore the Community

We have covered a lot of topics in the book, and I hope I have given you a good introduction to many of them. That doesn't mean you have to stop exploring any of them. You might have wanted to know more about stereotypes, the trans umbrella or the way that we're all evolving.

We don't just learn at school or from books. We can learn every day of our lives – I still learn new things, and I am grateful for it. So as you move through the journey of you, and come to know the community more, allow your understanding of it to grow. Explore the magical community that you are part of. There is so much for you to learn and share.

The people I shared with you in the last section could be a great place for you to start. You could research each of them and see how they have changed the world. This will lead you to other people who can inspire you. The whole community is there ready for you to discover and, big or small, it can have a huge impact on you if you let it!

Celebrate YOU!

I love a birthday – because it is one of the few days where you get to celebrate yourself. People treasure special occasions – because they don't happen every day. I am not so sure this is true. When it comes to you, you are a special occasion – and being you happens every day.

I am not saying you need to blow out candles and eat cake every day! Instead you need to remember all that you are – and how amazing that is. There is no one quite like you – and this should be celebrated. When we treat ourselves with the respect that special occasions deserve, we are boosting our self-worth – which helps others see how wonderful we are.

We have discussed all the ways that it might be hard to be us right now. Celebrating who you are on a daily basis is a beautiful way to prove doubtful people wrong. So, however you want to, celebrate you everyday. Be joyful that you are yourself. You have your unique perspective on the world – and no one can take that away from you. Never forget that you are a special occasion.

Role Model: Bimini (they/them)

Non-binary drag icon Bimini burst into our world through our TVs on *Drag Race UK*. Bimini – the stage name of Tommy Hibbitts – has gone on to be a hugely successful model, performer, musician and best-selling author. They have managed to shine a huge light on the non-binary community in a very positive way – and they represent the trans community with grace and elegance.

Speaking to the *Evening Standard*, Bimini offered advice to their teenage self:

It's okay that you don't feel you fit in right now or you don't know where you're going. There are no right or wrong answers. I hope there are more people coming out now for the younger generation to look up to because when I was growing up, gay or queer people were all stereotypical. Now they're a lot more diverse.[12]

It is clear that we will be seeing more from Bimini as they continue to be a huge chunk of representation for the trans community — as well as educating allies. We are very lucky to have an icon like Bimini in our lives!

Key Takeaways from this Chapter

- ♥ Being kind to yourself is an act of personal allyship — you deserve it!
- ♥ Time is our friend! Time will allow us all to be who we are, so let it take your hand and you will grow every day.
- ♥ You are exactly who you feel you are — and I want you to hold on to that.
- ♥ There are billions of people on the planet — and yet there is only one you.
- ♥ We are all evolving every day — so why rush it, when it will happen very nicely on its own?!
- ♥ In the LGBTQIA+ community there are countless people we can all look up to — and learn from.
- ♥ We never stop learning.
- ♥ Our self-worth will help others respect us.
- ♥ Never forget that you are a special occasion.

What Next? Crossword

There was a lot to digest and think about in this last chapter. So I thought a crossword might be a great way to use the knowledge you have just taken in.

Use the descriptions below to figure out which term or word fits. It's okay if you need to flip back over the last few pages to help you answer them – you're still learning! Have fun...

Across

3. There is only one you – you're...
5. Being friendly, generous and considerate
7. Explore the community and you can...
8. People to look up to

Down

1. You need...to grow
2. The opposite of taking things slow
4. Prove doubtful people wrong
6. You don't need to be visible to be...

Chapter 12
Things I Wish I Knew

G rowing up is not the easiest thing for many people. In fact, for a lot of us, it can be very hard, confusing and frustrating. If it wasn't hard enough dealing with all those emotions, some of you may be tackling this alone.

I am sure that throughout this book you will have had lots of thoughts swirling around your head. I wish we could sit down together and discuss everything. Having a reassuring conversation with someone who has gone through similar things to you can be so helpful, reassuring and comforting.

I can't offer you that exactly, but I can offer you the next best thing. In this chapter, I have asked some truly wonderful people from the LGBTQIA+ community to share some words with you. I hope their words will act as a comfort to you, and show you that being yourself is truly wonderful.

In this chapter we will:

- Explore advice from some amazing LGBTQIA+ community members.
- Get to grips with advice they wish they had been given – but are now giving to you!
- Focus on the things we can all worry about less.
- Oh, and, of course, we can't forget about the importance of always learning from other people!

Dani St James, she/her – founder of the charity Not A Phase and trans specialist brand Zoah

Q: What advice would you give your younger self?

A: It's very easy when you look around and you can't see yourself reflected in the vision of others, to feel that you don't belong. My advice to you would be to not emulate others in an attempt to belong. You are perfect the way you are. You are going to take so many forms as you grow and change. Trust the process and take the pressure off of yourself. You have a moral compass inside of you that is guided by all of the love and lessons that you have absorbed along the way; it is going to keep guiding you on your journey.

Q: What do you wish you knew then, that you know now?

A: That there was a whole world full of people that would understand, accept and celebrate me. I was raised in a place and at a time where there was no communication outside of my little bubble; now with the way that the world is, it is so much easier to find your people. My goodness, did I find mine! A shared feeling of displacement brings our community together. Sometimes it takes a bus or a train or an aeroplane, but when we find each other, magic happens. It was waiting for me and it is waiting for you, too, just as soon as you are ready.

Q: What do you wish you spent less time worrying about?

A: That I would never find love, as a trans person without representation of other trans people in traditional relationships; I thought that love was off the cards for me. I couldn't have been more wrong, I have been lucky enough to love lots of people in lots of different ways over the years and also to fall madly in love with my partner in recent years. The lesson here is that abso-lutely nothing is off the cards for you sweetheart, whether what you dream of is to do a certain job or, like me, fall in love. Whatever it is, you are capable and you will do it.

Georgie Tyrone, they/he – non-binary model and content creator

Q: What advice would you give your younger self?

A: You, my dear, will be okay. In fact, you will be more than okay. Find love for yourself. Make peace with yourself. Don't listen to the bullies. Pay little attention to the names. You are a very unique and special human, and that makes you awesome.

Q: What do you wish you knew then, that you know now?

A: There is nothing wrong with you. Absolutely nothing at all. All the things people point out as reasons why they think you are not 'normal' are the things that will become your superpowers. So be kind to yourself and don't be too hard on yourself.

Q: What do you wish you spent less time worrying about?

A: Fear and rejection. The fear of being bullied, the fear of people not liking me, the fear of not fitting in, the fear of walking a certain way, or preferring certain toys. The fear that our communities will reject us, especially for black and brown kids. But I want to reassure you, that you are not alone; as you grow you will find your people, you will make amazing like-minded friends. Don't worry about people who don't like you; they are missing out on how special you are.

Max Slack, he/they – trans
LGBTQIA+ activist, consultant and creator

Q: What advice would you give your younger self?

A: You're different, and that's okay. In fact, it'll become your greatest strength. I know right now all you want is to fit in; I know you want to look just like the other people at school. I know you want to be interested in the things they like which just don't make sense to you, and to be welcomed into their groups. It's okay to fake it sometimes, but remember that your differences make you unique and interesting. They'll be the reason why you thrive as an adult. Soon you will meet people who are different, too, and they'll celebrate you. One day far away, your uniqueness, your 'weird interests', will take you to places you don't even know about yet. The difficulties you have connecting with other people right now will teach you how to engage with anyone and everyone.

Q: What do you wish you knew then, that you know now?

A: You don't have to follow a set path. There's a very strict structure in place in the universe around you right now, but you will grow up and leave and see there are all sorts of options for how to live your life.

Q: What do you wish you spent less time worrying about?

A: I wish I'd spent less time worrying about what people thought of me, my choices and the way I presented myself to the world. I wish I'd realized sooner that if you're choosing to live your happiest, most authentic life, and someone doesn't support that choice, that's on them, not you. It's okay to take into consideration the opinions of people who love and support you, but if you don't think they understand you or have your best interests at heart, it's okay to disagree and choose your own way.

Iesha Palmer, they/them – LGBTQIA+ activist and Campaigns Officer at the charity Mermaids

Q: What advice would you give your younger self?

A: You may feel lonely, but you're not alone. There is nothing wrong with how you're feeling, and even though you don't have the language to explain, your existence is valid and valued. Believe in yourself a little bit more; hold yourself a little tighter. Know it's not about things getting better. It's about you caring less about what other people think.

Q: What do you wish you knew then, that you know now?

A: The people who ridicule and criticize who you are, it's never really about you! It's about their own discomfort they feel when they see someone living authentically. A lot of shame and guilt I was carrying wasn't even mine to carry in the first place.

Q: What do you wish you spent less time worrying about?

A: Other people's opinions! So much of it didn't come from a place of love and care. It came from a place of fear and control.

Annie Wade Smith, they/she — youth worker, plus size model and LGBTQIA+ activist

Q: What advice would you give your younger self?

A: I know sometimes you might feel like the odd one out and that nobody really understands you. You might feel like you don't have lots of friends like you. There's a huge world out there just waiting for you where you will meet people like you and you will feel safe, accepted and unique.

Q: What do you wish you knew then, that you know now?

A: Sometimes people say hurtful things, but that's because they don't understand, that's because they want to dull your sparkle. Sometimes when you sparkle other people are mean because they don't know how to sparkle like you. In life, aim to encourage others to shine with you, because embracing your sparkle is a wonderful thing!

Q: What do you wish you spent less time worrying about?

A: You don't have to know everything about who you are just yet. There's life lessons. There's learning. There's meeting new people! The only thing you have to do is to follow your heart and your dreams, and do what feels right for you. I believe in you. You are magical!

Yassine Senghor, she/her – Equalities, Diversity and Inclusion specialist

Q: What advice would you give your younger self?

A: You're gonna be okay. No, better than okay. You're gonna be kind of great! Things can get really tough, and sometimes, even when you are surrounded by people, you might feel alone and like no one gets you. But you are kind and generous and caring and compassionate and really very funny, even if no one laughs at your jokes! Don't let anyone take those things away from you or make you feel like there's something wrong with you. There are people out there who have felt how you feel, and they will really see you, just as you are. They will make you feel safe and like you are enough. No, more than enough – great!

Q: What do you wish you knew then, that you know now?

A: I wish I knew that it was okay to ask for help. Even as a kid, because I was a 'girl' I was always told I had to look after everyone else. That usually meant putting other people first and not looking after myself. I wish I had known that I don't have to take care of everyone else all the time. I wish I had known that it was okay to say that I was scared, or sad, or lonely, and that sometimes I needed someone to look after me. Maybe then, I would then have been able to learn to look after myself too (don't worry, I just about know how to now, but only because I finally learned how to ask for help!).

Q: What do you wish you spent less time worrying about?

A: I wish I'd spent less time worrying that I was bad or letting people down or that there was something wrong with me. Lots of not so great things have happened to me, but they didn't happen because of me or because there was something wrong with me. I'm different from a lot of people, and sometimes I struggle with things or feel down, but there is nothing wrong with that and there is absolutely *nothing* wrong with me.

Michael Edward Stephens, he/they – founder and CEO of We Create Space

Q: What advice would you give your younger self?

A: Don't always try to be the person you think others will like or find funny. It's exhausting, and can create a barrier to true connection, and love. Focus instead on being the kind of person you want to be. Focus on your creativity and kindness. This is where you will have the opportunity to explore and connect more fully with yourself, and others.

Q: What do you wish you knew then, that you know now?

A: I wish I knew that those difficult moments would eventually pass. That I wasn't alone. That I was loved. And that everything would, in the end, all be okay.

Q: What do you wish you spent less time worrying about?

A: *Everything!* But mainly how I looked. The hours spent worrying about appearance and how I was being seen by others. I overthought everything! Was I being too camp, too flamboyant, *too gay*?! It has taken a long time but now I believe that you can never be 'too much' of any of these things. Yes, not everyone will understand or appreciate it, but we must not limit ourselves and our potential based on the 'rules' others try to put on us.

Coco Tucker, she/they – creative writer, poet, speaker and mental health advocate

Q: What advice would you give your younger self?

A: I always ask myself and everyone around me this: to my younger self I'd tell you to continue to be strong and to be wiser in certain situations. Continue to be your true self. Show up to the world exactly as you want. Don't follow what society says you should do.

Q: What do you wish you knew then, that you know now?

A: I wish you knew that greatness would be my fate, that I would be here inspiring people around the world. Tearing up stereotypes that caused me so much pain, growing up.

Q: What do you wish you spent less time worrying about?

A: I guess when it comes to worrying less, it's always about what others think of me. I was always concerned about what others thought. I so desperately wanted to be accepted. Well, not any more!

Ellen Jones, she/her – Diversity, Equality and Inclusion specialist and autism activist, campaigner, speaker and writer

Q: What advice would you give your younger self?

A: I was bullied horrendously growing up, especially for being gay, and I found it really difficult to see myself as someone worth investing in. I would tell my younger self that I am important and that I deserve to be cared for and looked after.

Q: What do you wish you knew then, that you know now?

A: There is a lot of advice that understandably places importance on fluidity or changing labels over time, and while that might be the case for some people, it was never an experience that I related to. I have been out as a lesbian since I was 14, and for almost a decade I have used the word 'lesbian' to describe myself. Having come out so young, there were definitely critics of the fact I so confidently and proudly identified myself. I wish I knew that not only is it okay to be certain of your identity from a young age, but that it is just as glorious and brilliant as those who change their labels or who find that their identity shifted. There is no ideal, linear path we should take, and part of our community's magic is in all the different paths we have trodden to reach the same place.

Q: What do you wish you spent less time worrying about?

A: I have spent nearly all of my life worrying about how I look and if other people are judging me. It's only in my twenties that I'm beginning to relinquish that shame, be bolder and take up more space. There are so many things I wouldn't do because of fear of how I looked, and I know I'm not alone in that. But there are more important things in life than the judgement of others.

Shiva Raichandani, they/them – performer, dancer, director, filmmaker and educator

Q: What advice would you give your younger self?

A: How you see yourself is more important than how others see you. Choosing yourself isn't selfish; it is necessary. Don't live to please others because you'll only end up drifting away from who you truly are, and sometimes, undoing that violence and finding your way back to yourself can be deeply challenging.

Q: What do you wish you knew then, that you know now?

A: Sometimes we get so distracted by holding on to a specific identity that we forget how complex and expansive we are as individuals, and just how hard it is to reduce ourselves to one specific label. Right from the moment we're born, we start constructing our identities in ways that help others make sense of us. Rarely do we then deconstruct those adopted identifiers of ourselves to really understand what makes sense *to us*. To simplify, think of it this way: we have so many labels attached to us based on various factors. We're identified as someone's – 'child', 'sibling', 'grandchild', 'student', 'friend'; we're identified based on our looks – 'the tall one', 'the one with long hair', 'the one with cute jumpers'; we're identified based on our skin colour, religion, sexuality, gender, speech, and so many other things. At any given point in time we're not just *one* of these things. And similarly, at different points of our life, not *all* of these identifiers hold true for us. We grow, some of our identifiers change with us, we adopt newer roles and labels, we drop some. And therein lies the bigger picture – that there is no need to attach to a particular label to be considered valid and/or to exist.

The aim now then, for me at least, is to understand that while labels are helpful and sometimes necessary in day-to-day life, we are so much more beyond them, and that our true selves will still exist without said labels. We can truly realize our potential by being aware of that. And there's immense comfort in knowing that truth.

Q: What do you wish you spent less time worrying about?

A: I wish I didn't worry too much about being (or fearing ending up) alone because I never truly was. I had ancestors who paved the way for me to find comfort in; I had people online – friends and television characters alike who supported me during turbulent times; and, more importantly, I had a beautiful community of trans and gender non-conforming comrades waiting to share their love with me. We're never truly alone; and honestly, it's life-affirming to know that.

Spencer Cooper, they/them – founder of Love Queers and co-host of the 'Queer Talk' podcast

Q: What advice would you give your younger self?

A: To my younger self I would say two things. Firstly, give yourself a break and secondly, give yourself some credit for that matter. Having to navigate a broken family, school, being misunderstood and body issues at such a young age is an incredibly admirable thing. You will conquer it all. You will find those who understand and who truly love you for you. There will come a time where you will feel so comfortable and confident in who you are and all of this will be nothing but a stepping stone to greatness. Patience and empathy are your greatest strengths, so lean into them and don't waste time on anything or anyone who disapproves.

Q: What do you wish you knew then, that you know now?

A: Less what and more who. My chosen family has been my inspiration, my education and my reason for living. This unbreakable bond is one I never expected to have and one that I couldn't be without. To have such a wide breadth of wisdom, knowledge and experience from such brilliant individuals has been a mutual exchange that I will be forever grateful for. Finding your tribe is difficult. But once you have them you will feel so safe and satisfied and nothing else will matter.

Q: What do you wish you spent less time worrying about?

A: Changing the world! There is an immense pressure to go out into the world and do something life-changing. My mantra has and always will be, to focus on those closer to home. If you can inform, educate and spread love among those around you, that ripple effect will be a lot more authentic and sincere. We can help ourselves and those around us. We do not need the pressure of fixing the world we live in. The fight is real, but it is one to be fought for together, not on our own.

Jude Guaitamacchi, they|them – public speaker, consultant, model and influencer

Q: What advice would you give your younger self?

A: I find the idea of giving my younger self advice difficult to understand. The world became such a painful place in ways I consider beyond my control. However, I can imagine giving myself words of affirmation and encouragement, letting myself know that I wasn't alone and that I had nothing to be ashamed of. I'd give myself hope, that things will get better and that one day I will experience joy and the freedom to be who I am.

Q: What do you wish you knew then, that you know now?

A: I wish I'd been taught LGBTQIA+ topics when I was at school and that I'd been given the terminology to be able to communicate my identity instead of just learning to be someone I wasn't and reject my true self. I wish I knew that I was lovable, worthy and I was always beautiful. I wish I knew that there were plenty of people just like me, a whole community, waiting for me with open arms.

Q: What do you wish you spent less time worrying about?

A: I wish I'd spent less time worrying about what everyone thought of me, fearing ridicule, being self-conscious and trying to mould myself into the version of who I thought the world wanted me to be. Realizing that the shame wasn't mine to carry, I gave myself permission to reveal the parts of myself I had been ashamed of. Over time the shame began to fade and I began to love and celebrate those parts of myself. I was able to empower myself and learn the path to true joy wasn't in the acceptance and validation of others, but in loving and embracing myself.

Reflect on Your Thoughts

Using the hand mirror below, you can reflect on your feelings after reading this chapter. How do you feel having heard other people's experiences? What feels different? Is there something that you feel better about? Is there anything you want to try and explore now...?

Chapter 13

Useful Resources

So we are coming to the close of the book, but I couldn't leave you without offering you further support and resources. I am well aware that we have covered a wide range of topics in this book. This may have answered some of your questions, but it might have created more. This is okay.

There is also a chance that this book might not have ticked all your boxes – this is also okay. I would like this to be one of the many resources that you have to help you be yourself. This book is your starting point. There is always more to learn and develop your understanding of.

In this chapter we will:

- Explore charities and organizations that can help you.
- Get to grips with some other books you can read.
- Focus on the many things you can use to educate yourself.
- Oh, and, of course, we can't forget about the importance of people to learn from!

Charities and Organizations

- Anxiety UK, Helpline 03444 775774/text 'support' to 07537 416905, www.anxietyuk.org.uk
  A user-led service for those who are struggling with stress and anxiety, this service is not LGBTQIA+ exclusive, but offers instant advice and help for those who are struggling. The Helpline is open Monday–Friday.

- CALM, Helpline 0800 585858, www.thecalmzone.net
  CALM (Campaign Against Living Miserably) is the leading movement to

prevent suicide. It offers a helpline and web chat service seven days a week to help those struggling with suicidal thoughts, and also a service for those affected by suicide. The Helpline is open 5pm–midnight, 365 days a year.

- Childline, Helpline 0800 1111, www.childline.org.uk
  A counselling service in the UK for children and young people up to their 19th birthday provided by the NSPCC. Offering support 24 hours a day, seven days a week – there is always someone for you to speak to.

- FFLAG, Helpline 0300 6880368, www.fflag.org.uk
  FFLAG is a national voluntary organization and charity dedicated to supporting families and their LGBTQIA+ loved ones.

- Gendered Intelligence, https://genderedintelligence.co.uk
  Gendered Intelligence runs projects for young people who identify as trans. It also has information for parents and families. A support line, 0330 3559678, is available at select times.

- Just Like Us, www.justlikeus.org
  Just Like Us is a charity that acknowledges that growing up LGBT+ is still unacceptably tough. It works with schools across the UK to improve the lives of LGBTQIA+ young people.

- Kidscape, https://kidscape.org.uk
  Kidscape is dedicated to helping young people affected by bullying. This service is not LGBTQIA+ exclusive, but offers support, training and advice to challenge bullying. A parent advice line is also offered.

- Kooth, www.kooth.com
  Kooth offers free anonymous mental health support, targeted at younger audiences. It also acts as a signposting service for other mental health services available across the UK.

- Mermaids, Helpline 0808 8010400, https://mermaidsuk.org.uk
  Mermaids supports transgender, non-binary and gender-diverse children,

young people and their families. Mermaids also operates an emergency text service; if you need help now, text 'Mermaids' to 85258.

- Mindline Trans+, Helpline 0300 330 5468, http://mindlinetrans.org.uk
  Mindline Trans+ is a UK-wide helpline and website run by and for trans, non-binary, gender-diverse and gender-fluid people. It offers a free, confidential, judgement-free service for support and advice, and its helpline is available at select times.

- NHS 111 service, https://111.nhs.uk
  Call 111 when you need medical help fast but it is not a 999 emergency. NHS 111 is available 24 hours a day, 365 days a year and is free to call. Help is also available via the website.

- Not A Phase, https://notaphase.org
  Supporting the lives of trans+ adults across the UK is the core message of Not A Phase, a small charity that is working towards a brighter future for the trans+ community.

- Papyrus, Helpline 0800 0684141/text 07860 039967/
  email pat@papyrus-uk.org, www.papyrus-uk.org
  Papyrus is a suicide prevention helpline for young people. Call, text or email Monday–Friday 10am–10pm, weekends 2pm–10pm.

- Samaritans, Helpline 116 123, www.samaritans.org
  Samaritans is a charity aimed at helping anyone in emotional distress. It has dedicated helplines and offers help for free whenever you need it.

- Shout, Text 'shout' to 85258, https://giveusashout.org
  Shout is the UK's free mental health text support service, which offers free, impartial advice every day of the year.

- Stonewall, Email info@stonewall.org.uk, www.stonewall.org.uk
  Full of information, resources and help. It also operates an information service. Open 9.30am–4.30pm Monday – Friday.

- SupportLine, Helpline 01708 765200/email info@supportline.org.uk, www.supportline.org.uk
  SupportLine is particularly aimed at those who are isolated, at risk, vulnerable and victims of any form of abuse. It offers confidential emotional support to children, young adults and adults by telephone, email and post.

- Switchboard, Helpline 0300 330 0630, https://switchboard.lgbt
  Switchboard offers a listening service via calls, email or messaging to help you. It covers all the intersections of mental health and is LGBTQIA specific, with all volunteers self-defining as LGBTQIA. Open 10am–10pm every day.

- The Proud Trust, www.theproudtrust.org
  An organization that helps young people empower themselves to make a positive change for themselves. With experiences, testimonials and web chat support.

- Young Minds, www.youngminds.org.uk
  Young Minds is the UK's leading mental health charity for young people. It has lots of resources online for young people and parents too.

Books

- *What's the T? The No-Nonsense Guide to All Things Trans and/or Non-Binary for Teens* – Juno Dawson
  This guide is angled at teenagers, presenting what it means to be transgender or non-binary in a frank and humorous way. Dawson offers advice on labels, identities, sex and relationships. She also includes her transgender and non-binary peers, to offer their individual advice and opinions.

- *Gender Explorers: Our Stories of Growing Up Trans and Changing the World* – Juno Roche
  In this collection of interviews with young transgender people, writer and campaigner Juno Roche brings an open and candid reflection of gender from a very fresh and modern angle.

- *Coming Out Stories: Personal Experiences of Coming Out from Across the LGBTQ+ Spectrum* – Emma Goswell and Sam Walker
  A powerful and uplifting collection of coming out stories from LGBTQ+ people. Here to inspire and uplift, this book helps you understand and learn from an intersectional array of coming out stories.

- *Trans Survival Workbook* – Owl and Fox Fisher
  Specifically aimed at those who are transitioning, this guide allows you to document and explore the relationship you have with yourself throughout the process of transitioning. It also has a focus on wellness and mental health.

- *Beyond the Gender Binary* – Alok Vaid-Menon
  In this mini-guide, writer and performer Alok Vaid-Menon urges you to see the gender spectrum in colour, asking you to see beyond transphobia that halts the progress of the community, allowing you to learn to celebrate yourself by living an authentic life.

- *Bottled: A Picture Book to Help Children Share Their Feelings* – Tom and Joe Brassington
  This small book packs a big punch, helping you learn how to effectively discuss

your feelings. As with many things in our lives, we can all feel the pressure, and try to bottle up how we feel. Tom and Joe Brassington are here to help you find other ways to express yourself.

- *The Book of Non-Binary Joy: Embracing the Power of You* – Ben Pechey
  I might be a bit biased, but if you want to explore non-binary identities, then this book might be the best one for you, helping you thrive as your authentic – and most fabulous – non-binary self. Packed full of personal stories, valuable insights and interactive sections, this inspiring book covers a wide range of topics, including mental health, pleasure, fashion, understanding your past, allyship privilege and self-expression.

- *You Can Make a Difference! A Creative Workbook and Journal for Young Activists* – Sherry Paris
  This fun and interactive guide is a great resource if you feel you want to make a difference in the world by creating change or even becoming an activist. This could be a great book for any up-and-coming change makers.

- *The Trans Self-Care Workbook: A Coloring Book and Journal for Trans and Non-Binary People* – Theo Lorenz
  This creative journal and workbook offers a unique take on celebrating transgender and non-binary identities. Through pages of colouring, journaling prompts, advice and space for self-reflection you can find a deeper understanding of your gender identity.

People

- Ki Griffin (he/they), actor and campaigner. They were the first non-binary and intersex actor to become a regular cast member in Channel 4's soap *Hollyoaks*.

- Alok Vaid-Menon (they/them), writer, performer and public speaker. Alok is an inspiring icon within the community. They use love and compassion in a way that unites us as a community, highlighting our strength together.

- Paris Lees (she/her), writer, presenter and columnist. Paris Lees is a trailblazer for the trans community. She was the first openly trans presenter on BBC Radio One and Channel 4, and has appeared in British *Vogue*.

- Travis Alabanza (they/them), award-winning writer, theatre maker and performance artist. Travis is a huge talent and cheerleader for the trans community – and is a true role model for all of us.

- Charlie Craggs (she/her), trans campaigner, writer, actress, icon and all-round queer hero. Charlie is a true hero in the community, creating change for all in her own unique style.

- Bimini (they/them), non-binary drag icon, model, performer, musician and best-selling author. Bimini, aka Tommy Hibbitts, shines a huge light on the non-binary community in a very positive way – and they represent the trans community with grace and elegance.

- Munroe Bergdorf (she/they), model, campaigner, author and podcaster. Munroe is a champion for the LGBTQIA+ community. In 2020 British *Vogue* named her in the top 25 most influential women in the country!

- Shon Faye (she/her), writer, editor, journalist and presenter. Shon has created a wonderful legacy of incredible writing and education for the trans community, notably her best-selling book *The Trans Issue*.

- Lady Phyll (she/her). Phyllis Akua Opoku-Gyimah, also known as Lady Phyll, is an activist and campaigner, and director and co-founder of UK Black Pride. She is also a tireless fighter for the rights of queer, trans and intersex people of colour in the UK and globally.

- Juno Roche (she/her), writer, campaigner and founder of Trans Workers UK and the Trans Teachers Network. Juno is one of Britain's best writers on LGBTQIA+ and trans-specific topics.

- Eva Echo (she/they), trans advocate, speaker, model and campaigner. Eva works tirelessly to improve the lives of trans and non-binary people. With such passion, Eva is well on the way to changing the world.

- Juno Dawson (she/her), writer, activist, screenwriter, journalist and actor. Juno is such an inspiring human, and has gone out of her way to lift and enrich the trans and LGBTQIA+ community at every stage of her career.

- Ugla Stefanía (they/them), trans activist, educator, author and filmmaker. Ugla is another one of our community's hardest workers. They have campaigned for trans rights for over a decade.

- Bobbi Pickard (she/her), trans activist and CEO of Trans in the City, an organization that brings together global organizations, corporates and companies to create inclusion for transgender, non-binary and gender diversity in business. Bobbi is a tireless advocate for our community, and is an incredible human.

- Dani St James (she/her), founder of the charity Not A Phase and trans specialist brand Zoah. Dani is a trans powerhouse, working tirelessly to improve the lives of trans people in the UK.

- Georgie Tyrone (they/he), aka Triple Minor, non-binary model and content creator. Georgie is a shining light of representation in the community, using creativity and fashion to inspire thousands.

- Max Slack (he/they), trans LGBTQIA+ activist, consultant, creator and wonderful human. Max pours joy into the word with their presence.

- Iesha Palmer (they/them), LGBTQIA+ activist and Campaigns Officer at the charity Mermaids. Iesha influences change and makes a difference through campaigning, and was instrumental in bringing the charity's podcast 'She Said, They Said' to life.

- Annie Wade Smith (they/she), youth worker, plus size model and LGBTQIA+ activist. Annie has such a positive presence in the world, and touches so many lives with her joy.

- Yassine Senghor (she/her), Equalities, Diversity and Inclusion specialist with expertise in LGBT inclusion and creating anti-racist spaces. Yassine is a powerhouse of change, with a passion for equality.

- Michael Edward Stephens (he/they), founder and CEO of We Create Space. Michael is a tireless advocate for queer people the world over, bringing queer people together in business and the wider world, creating space for us all.

- Coco Tucker (she/they), creative writer, poet, speaker and mental health activist. Coco is a huge advocate for queer humans with a focus on those who are neurodivergent.

- Ellen Jones (she/her), Diversity, Equality and Inclusion specialist and autism activist, campaigner, speaker and writer. Ellen's work focuses on building inclusion and equality for LGBTQIA+ people and disabled people across the globe.

- Shiva Raichandani (they/them), performer, dancer, director, filmmaker and educator. Shiva uses dance as a form of story-telling. They have featured on *Britain's*, *India's* and *France's Got Talent* and are so talented!

- Spencer Cooper (they/them), founder of Love Queers and co-host of the 'Queer Talk' podcast. Spencer is a huge believer in community, and works tirelessly to bring awareness, acceptance and success to all they meet in their work.

- Jude Guaitamacchi (they/them), public speaker, consultant, model and influencer. Jude works tirelessly to be the role model that they didn't have when they were growing up. They champion trans inclusion across the world of fashion, beauty, education and business.

- Fox Fisher (they/he), trans activist, educator, author and filmmaker. Fox is another one of our community's hardest workers. They have campaigned for trans rights for over a decade.

- Dr Ronx Ikharia (they/them), trans non-binary A&E doctor. Dr Ronx is everything we need in modern healthcare. They educate in all that they do and give me faith that services we access are beginning to adapt to the lives we live.

- Tanya Compas (she/her), youth worker and campaigner. Tanya works tirelessly for the black queer community, and makes such a difference to so many lives.

People Who Are There for You

You can use this space to jot down any of the trusted grown-ups, friends or family members you can turn to. When you need them, your list will be here for you – which you may just find helpful on a more difficult day...

. . . .

. . . .

. . . .

. . . .

This Isn't Goodbye Really

I don't like goodbyes. I never have, and I never will. However, we are at the final part of the book. It would be a perfect time to say goodbye. Except I won't, because goodbye is the wrong word for you. Instead the word you need is *hello!* Hello to your future, your life, and all of the amazing things I know you are going to achieve.

We have talked about difference a lot. How difference can be scary to others. How difference can be used against us. As this is the last part of the book where we are together, I think it is important, most of all, for me to remind you to never be scared of difference. Never be scared that you think you aren't like everyone else. This is your superpower.

You are what makes you incredible – nothing else. The fact that you may have been left to feel less than special in the past is a reflection of the world around you. This has nothing to do with who you are as a person. We are all different. Your uniqueness will make your life wonderful, and I hope you hold on to it, and treasure who you are.

Just because your gender is perhaps a little different to the expectations of those around you doesn't make it any less valid. It doesn't make you small, and it doesn't mean you deserve less. You are special, and not just celebrated in the pages of this book – but pretty soon so many people are going to get to know you, and love you for who you are – no questions asked!

The brilliant thing by getting to the end of this book is that you have already learned so much (unless you have decided to sneak a peak at the end, and then get back to the beginning!). Don't worry if you can't remember everything that you have read. First, because you can read it again if you want to – there is nothing stopping you! Second, I am here to remind you of some of the key areas and points we covered, in a handy list:

- Gender is confusing, and that's okay.
- Gender, sex and sexuality are all different – but they also overlap.
- Gender is how you feel.
- Sex is about your body parts.
- Sexuality is who you like.
- Gender identities are a big thing – and it's okay to be overwhelmed.
- Gender is made up – so you only need to please yourself!
- A pronoun is how we describe ourselves.
- Pronouns can be confusing, and that's okay.
- Pronouns are different for different people – it's a personal choice.
- It's respectful to ask people their pronouns.
- With perspective, big questions don't feel so big.
- Thinking about who you want to be is a good place to start.
- Other people can be difficult – this is not your fault.
- Working out who you are can take a long time – this is okay.
- Questioning is a helpful word if you haven't fully worked out your gender identity yet.
- Repeat after me: 'I am perfect'.
- Being part of the LGBTQIA+ community can be isolating – but it is not just you – you are never alone!
- You're not alone; you just might not have the right people around you yet!
- If others are being tricky, remember that the magical nature of being you has yet to reach them.
- Being 'different' is no bad thing.
- Clothing has no gender!
- Your clothes can act as an advert for acceptance.
- No one has the right to be horrible to another person based on their gender identity or expression.
- Some responses to LGBTQIA+ people are caused by prehistoric behaviour.

- We can't be happy all the time – and that's okay!
- Mental health doesn't just affect our head, but our bodies too.
- Other people can always help you – don't suffer in silence.
- Allies are people who support the beliefs of another group of people – and try to help!
- We don't need to be upset that we don't know everything – we're human!
- It's okay to get things wrong – mistakes are good!
- Being kind to yourself is an act of personal allyship – you deserve it!
- Time is our friend! Time will allow us all to be who we are.
- You are exactly who you feel you are – and I want you to hold on to that.

I am very aware that your experiences, life and circumstance may be drastically different to the ones we have discussed here. This may mean that this book has not hit the mark for you – this is okay! We are all different, so we all need different resources to help us. Use the books, people and organizations listed in Chapter 13 to guide you if you feel you need it.

So here we are, the end of the book, but the beginning of the rest of your life. As I said, I won't say goodbye; I want to remind you to celebrate yourself every day – because you are a special occasion, and never forget it!

Acknowledgements

Acknowledgements are always the last thing on your mind when you begin writing. While writing a book is a lonely pursuit, it is never completed alone. There are so many wonderful people who have been on this journey with me.

First I have to thank Andrew at Jessica Kingsley Publishers for believing in me to create this resource. It is such a privilege to be able to sit at my computer and share my words, knowing they will end up in an actual book! I am still pinching myself that this is my second book – maybe I am good at this after all?!

This book was written during some really difficult life events. I owe the world to my mum Ruth, and sister Rachel who did so much to keep me on track and able to complete this project. Life isn't always easy, and I am not sure I would have coped without you. Thank you doesn't really cover just how grateful I am – I owe you both my life.

To mum, I also owe another thanks, for all the help you provided during the editing phase. I never would have been able to put all the pieces together if it wasn't for your patience, support and experience with younger readers. Thank you for managing to cope with me *again* – can't wait to work together in the future!

To my professional family, the team at Tape, thank you for guiding me through the ever-confusing world of work we currently exist in.

Thank you to Dani, Georgie, Max, Iesha, Annie, Yassine, Michael, Coco, Ellen, Shiva, Spencer and Jude for lending your powerful words to me, and for allowing me to pass them on to the readers of this book.

I also want to thank Emily, my therapist. Having you as an outlet, and safe place to explore the inner workings of my mind, has made me a better person, and ultimately led to the creation of this wonderful book. I highly recommend Self Space when it comes to your therapy needs.

Thank you Sam for the illustrations, which bring my words to life. Working with you on this book has been such a pleasure – thank you for sharing your talent with my readers once again!

I want to take the time to extend my thanks to all of the wonderful people who worked tirelessly behind the scenes on this book:

Abbie Howard (editorial assistant)
Adam Peacock (typesetter)
Andrew James (commissioning editor)
Claire Robinson (production editor)
Dawn Rushen (copyeditor)
Eliza Wright (proofreader)
Giuliana Di Mitrio (production controller)
Kara McHale (cover designer)

Finally I would like to thank all the people who support me in my world of work. Whether that is a reader, online follower, a PR at a brand, the person who books me for a job – I am grateful for all that you do. I am here as a voice of reason because of your support and belief in me, and I never take that for granted.

Puzzle and Questions Solutions

Chapter 1

Gender, Sex and Sexuality Quiz – Answers
1b. The way we feel, as a person
Our gender is the way we feel, as a person.

2c. At birth
Our sex is assigned at birth.

3a. Define you
Your assigned sex does not define you.

4c. Hegemony and heteronormativity
Hegemony and heteronormativity make it harder for LGBTQIA+ people to be supported.

5b. You
You are in charge of your gender, sex and sexuality – so have fun with it!

Chapter 2

Gender Identities Crossword – Solution

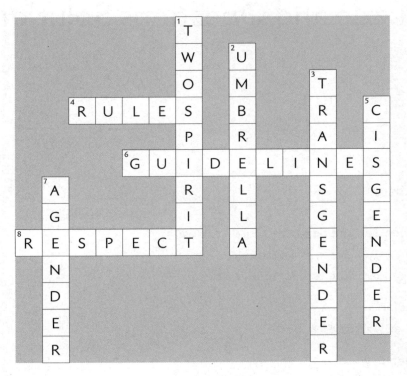

Across

4. Rules
6. Guidelines
8. Respect

Down

1. Two-Spirit
2. Umbrella
3. Transgender
5. Cisgender
7. Agender

Chapter 4

Question Time Word Search – Solution

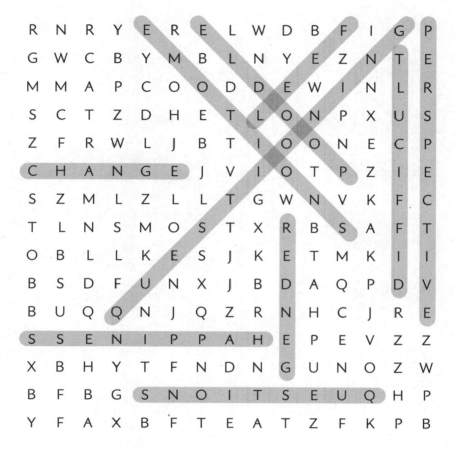

QUESTIONS   POODLE   GENDER
QUESTIONING   CHANGE
EMOTIONS   PERSPECTIVE   FEEL
HAPPINESS   DIFFICULT

Chapter 5

Complete the Sentences – Answers

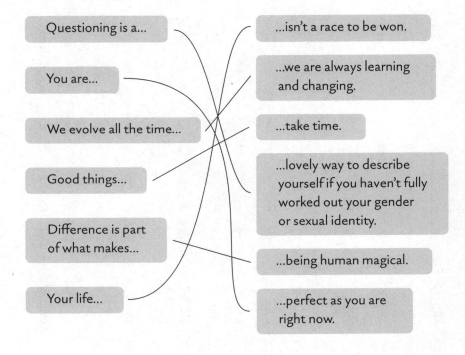

Questioning is a...

You are...

We evolve all the time...

Good things...

Difference is part of what makes...

Your life...

...isn't a race to be won.

...we are always learning and changing.

...take time.

...lovely way to describe yourself if you haven't fully worked out your gender or sexual identity.

...being human magical.

...perfect as you are right now.

Chapter 7

Fashion Help! – Solution

Janice (she/her)
Wants some fancy party shoes to feel fun and smart

Sasha (they/she)
Wants to explore more fitted structured garments

Fred (they/them)
Wants practical clothes for every day that allows them to move freely

Chapter 8

Barriers Quiz – Answers
1b. Fight or flight
Fight or flight is a reaction to new things.

2a. Visibility
A lack of visibility makes it very hard for us to feel like we have a place to belong.

3c. Fact
Transphobia is not fact, it's just opinions.

4a. Rite of passage
Bullying is not a rite of passage – and should not be accepted.

5b. Section 28
Section 28 was scrapped in 2003 in Wales and England, after being scrapped in 2000 in Scotland.

Chapter 10

Supportive Friend Guess Who – Solution

Chapter 11

What Next? Crossword – Solution

Across

3. Unique
5. Kindness
7. Learn
8. Elders

Down

1. Time
2. Rushing
4. Celebrate
6. Valid

Notes

1   Taken from www.teenvogue.com/story/lizzo-music-issue (accessed 11/07/2022).

2   Taken from www.thesun.co.uk/tv/13514919/hollyoaks-ki-griffin-intersex-non-binary-actor (accessed 11/07/2022).

3   Taken from https://public.oed.com/blog/a-brief-history-of-singular-they (accessed 11/07/2022).

4   Taken from www.dazeddigital.com/life-culture/article/51982/1/the-world-according-to-indya-moore-interview (accessed 11/07/2022).

5   Taken from www.biography.com/news/marsha-p-johnson-quotes (accessed 11/07/2022).

6   Taken from www.gq-magazine.co.uk/culture/article/billy-porter-interview (accessed 11/07/2022).

7   Taken from www.npg.org.uk/whatson/wearing-cahun/home (accessed 11/07/2022).

8   Taken from www.forbes.com/sites/dawnstaceyennis/2022/03/14/alok-is-searching-for-everyday-miracles-to-heal-broken-hearts-including-their-own/?sh=3cff937c1b42 (accessed 11/07/2022).

9   Taken from www.them.us/story/paris-lees-what-it-feels-like-for-a-girl-interview (accessed 11/07/2022).

10 Taken from www.refinery29.com/en-gb/2017/08/166568/travis-alabanza-before-i-step-outside (accessed 11/07/2022).

11 Taken from www.dazeddigital.com/life-culture/article/40213/1/charlie-craggs-nailtransphobia-trans-activist-the-finger-film (accessed 11/07/2022).

12 Taken from www.standard.co.uk/insider/bimini-bon-boulash-drag-race-es-magazine-interview-b936087.html (accessed 11/07/2022).

The Book of Non-Binary Joy

Embracing the Power of You
Ben Pechey
Illustrated by Sam Prentice

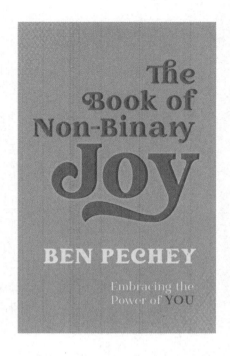

Whether you are at the start of your journey or have been on the wild ride of gender introspection for a long time, this guide is here to help you thrive as your authentic – and most fabulous – non-binary self. With personal stories, valuable insights and interactive sections, this inspiring book covers a wide range of topics, including mental health, pleasure, fashion, understanding your past, allyship privilege and self-expression. Written with warmth and unapologetic humour, and with bold illustrations throughout, Ben Pechey has created the ultimate safe space for you to embrace your non-binary life and start living.

Ben Pechey is a non-binary writer, presenter and fashion icon. They have written and produced content for *The Guardian*, *Cosmopolitan*, *Women's Health*, *Refinery29* and worked with a range of leading brands to educate and improve awareness of the LGBTQIA+ community. *The Book of Non-Binary Joy* is their first book.

£12.99 | $18.95 | PB | 224PP | ISBN 978 1 78775 910 7 | EISBN 978 1 78775 911 4

It's Totally Normal!

An LGBTQIA+ Guide to Puberty,
Sex, and Gender
*Monica Gupta Mehta
and Asha Lily Mehta*
Illustrated by Fox Fisher

Mother and teen duo Monica and Asha Mehta work together to answer your most pressing sex questions. Forget the penis-in-vagina basics—this is a queer-friendly guide that'll have you rethinking the very definition of sex. Combining expert advice with the personal experiences of teens all over the world, prepare to plunge into the topics they don't cover in sex ed. Masturbation, pornography, fetishes—if you're not afraid to ask, they're not afraid to answer.

Monica Gupta Mehta is a panromantic and demisexual parent, sex education and SEL teacher, and educational psychologist.

Asha Lily Mehta is her nonbinary, lesbian child, and together they are co-founders of Normalizers—an organization that seeks to provide education and support for LGBTQIA+ and autistic youth. Normalizers began on TikTok and now has more than 100,000 followers.

£12.99 | $18.95 | PB | 208PP | ISBN 978 1 83997 355 0 | EISBN 978 1 83997 356 7

Perfectly Queer

An Illustrated Introduction
Victoria Barron

The alphabet mafia? The queer umbrella? A little confused by—or curious about—the terminology and identities that make up the LGBTQIA+ community? For allies and queer folks alike, this visual introduction uses bright and fabulous illustrations to explain the rainbow of gender identities and sexualities. Activity pages—featuring a rainbow mascot, The Rain-boa Constrictor—divide chapters on gender identity, assigned sex, sexual and romantic orientations, acronyms, and common queer-ies, to make things (hopefully) more perfectly queer!

Victoria Barron (she/her) is an illustrator who identifies with a variety of LGBTQ+ labels and is a self-proclaimed 'queer weirdo' (or would that be 'q-weirdo'?). She enjoys creating works that make people smile, often applying a fun twist to themes of self-worth, acceptance, education, and awareness. Many of her works can be found via her Instagram account: @victoriabarronart, or website: www.victoriabarron.com.

£9.99 | $14.95 | PB | 96PP | ISBN 978 1 83997 408 3 | EISBN 978 1 83997 409 0

LGBTQIA+ Pride Sticker Book

Illustrated by Ollie Mann

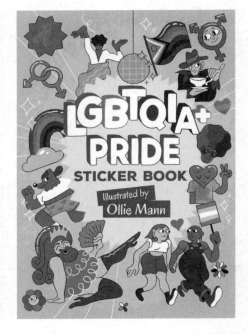

Bold, bright and fabulous just like you! This vibrant sticker book includes 200+ Pride themed stickers, featuring rainbows, Pride flags, pronouns and empowering slogans, all beautifully illustrated to be a source of inspiration, whether you're gay, bi, queer, intersex, trans, non-binary or an ally.

Stick a rainbow on your laptop, a slogan on your water bottle or a Pride symbol in your journal, these stickers are a colourful and powerful reminder to take pride in yourself and the LGBTQIA+ community.

Ollie Mann is an illustrator based in London who loves to create colourful cartoons that celebrate the queer community and beyond.

£8.99 | $14.95 | PB | 48PP | ISBN 978 1 83997 246 1

Queer Body Power

Finding Your Body Positivity
Essie Dennis

Inviting you to challenge accepted beauty standards and the concept of 'the perfect body', Essie takes everything they have learned on their journey to self-acceptance and body satisfaction to help guide you towards loving your queer body. From gender, sexuality and reclaiming your body, through to food, politics, social media and fatphobia, and with powerful stories from a diverse range of queer people throughout, this inspiring and necessary book will show you that you are enough.

Essie Dennis is a queer activist and writer. As a plus-size model they promote body positivity through their popular social media channels and have written widely on queer mental health and body image. Queer Body Power is their first book.

£14.99 | $19.95 | PB | 224PP | ISBN 978 1 78775 904 6 | EISBN 978 1 78775 905 3